SPEAKING OF SPEECH *Premium Edition*

Charles LeBeau

Basic Presentation Skills for Beginners

NATIONAL GEOGRAPHIC
LEARNING

JN116672

Australia · Brazil · Mexico · Singapore · United Kingdom · United States

Speaking of Speech, Premium Edition—Basic Presentation Skills for Beginners

Charles LeBeau

© 2021 Charles LeBeau

Photo Credits:
cover: © IAN S FOULK/National Geographic Image Collection; 11 (mt): © SweetBabeeJay/iStock.com; 13 (r): © Abbie Parr/Getty Images Sport/Getty Imges; 19 (t, mb): © july7th/iStock.com; 21 (m): © pabradyphoto/iStock.com; 23 (tlr): © Ross Gilmore/Getty Images Entertainment/Getty Images, (trr): © jack-sooksan/iStock.com, (bl): © 400tmax/iStock.com, (brl): © LoweStock/iStock.com, (brr): © RobynPhoto/iStock.com; 31 (tl): © Qvasimodo/iStock.com, (tm): © VectorStory/iStock.com, (tr): © pijama61/iStock.com, (ml): © Irina Cheremisinova/iStock.com, (mm): © Arctic-stock/iStock.com, (mr): © SHIROKUMA DESIGN/iStock.com, (bl): © robuart/iStock.com, (bm): © OlgaLIS/iStock.com, (br): © arata/iStock.com; 33 (tl): © monkeybusinessimages/iStock.com, (tm): © baona/iStock.com, (tr): © zhudifeng/iStock.com, (ml): © Jonathan W. Cohen/iStock.com, (mm): © Explora_2005/iStock.com, (mr): © southtownboy/iStock.com, (bl): © tomazl/iStock.com, (bm): © mizoula/iStock.com, (br): © winhorse/iStock.com; 36 (t): © londoneye/iStock.com, (m): © m-imagephotography/iStock.com, (b): © GlobalStock/iStock.com; 40 (3): © zhudifeng/iStock.com, (5): © wideonet/iStock.com; 41 (1): Courtesy of the U.S. Department of Energy Atmospheric Radiation Measurement (ARM) user facility, (2): © Handout/Getty Images Sport/Getty Images, (4): © Derek Brumby/iStock.com, (5): © Auscape/Universal Images Group/Getty Images; 44 (t): © Phynart Studio/iStock.com; 49 (t): © LeManna/iStock.com, (mt): © kckate16/iStock.com, (mm): © champlifezy@gmail.com/iStock.com, (mb): © simonkr/iStock.com; 50 (all): © NicoElNino/iStock.com; 55 (t): © AwaylGl/iStock.com; 57 (t): © JovanaMilanko/iStock.com, (b): © fcafotodigital/iStock.com; 67 (tr, mr, br): ©Barks_japan/iStock.com; 76: © michal_staniewski/iStock.com; 77: © Teacherdad48/iStock.com; 80 (3ml): © damircudic/iStock.com, (3mr): © valentinrussanov/iStock.com; 86 (t): © rabbit75_ist/iStock.com, (b): © Jack Hollingsworth/Photodisc/Getty Images; 87: © JAMES P. BLAIR/National Geographic Image Collection; 88: © zjzpp163/iStock.com; 101 (bl): © Tashi-Delek/iStock.com; 111 (bl): © yayayoyo/iStock.com

Unless noted above, all photos are from this textbook's video program: © Cengage Learning K.K.

For permission to use material from this textbook or product, e-mail to **eltjapan@cengage.com**

ISBN: 978-4-86312-385-4

National Geographic Learning | Cengage Learning K.K.
No. 2 Funato Building 5th Floor
1-11-11 Kudankita, Chiyoda-ku
Tokyo 102-0073
Japan

Tel: 03-3511-4392
Fax: 03-3511-4391

Contents

About This Book

This is the story of *Speaking of Speech*. And, if you are reading this, then you are part of that story.

Speaking of Speech started as a dream, on the back of a napkin. (I still have the napkin.) David Harrington and I used to relax in the lounge of the Yamato Grand Hotel in the late 1980's and doodle ideas for a presentation book on napkins. I kept the napkins. Just in case.

Several years later, feeling in a rut as I trudged home after work, I wished to myself that I could do something different, something exciting. That night, David called and asked if I still had the napkins because a publisher was interested in doing a presentation book.

We signed the contract with that publisher and were assigned an editor. Shortly afterwards, the editor quit (not our fault!), and David and I were left to fend for ourselves. We designed the book ourselves. We found a Canadian artist with an iconic style we really liked and contracted him to do the illustrations and the cover, which gave the first edition its unique feel.

It took us three years of Saturdays and holidays to finish.

The first edition of *Speaking of Speech* debuted in 1996. It was black and white and looked different than anything else on the market—a big risk. But it worked. You liked it.

The next edition of *Speaking of Speech* arrived in 2009—more than a decade later. This time, it was in color and came with a DVD shot in New York. Again, you liked it.

In January of 2020, our publisher, Macmillan, pulled up stakes and left Japan, making *Speaking of Speech* an orphan. National Geographic Learning has kindly adopted it and given it new life as *Speaking of Speech, Premium Edition*.

So, what is "premium" about the latest edition?

1. **The video has been re-shot and updated.**
   The new video bids farewell to the beloved characters of the first DVD and welcomes a new cast of characters. An episode featuring online presentations reflects the

new reality of the pandemic. Another new episode focuses on explaining visuals, a perennial problem all presenters face. Merwyn Torikian, our brilliant director and producer, has labored to make each episode entertaining, and has added new music and sophisticated animation to give the video some modern flash. New slides for each episode showcase the importance of the visual message.

2. **The textbook has been updated with key additions.**
   The earlier editions of *Speaking of Speech* focused on the three messages (the Physical Message, the Visual Message, and the Story Message), but little attention was given to the actual language of presentation—the Verbal Message. In the *Premium Edition*, we added the Verbal Message to provide the language scaffolding needed by non-native presenters to implement the other three messages successfully. Each unit now includes a section highlighting language specific to that unit's presentation. In addition, a new section on slide design is included in each unit to pre-empt the common pitfalls we so often see novice slide designers fall into. On some pages, we have taken advantage of National Geographic's extensive library of images to replace older illustrations with vivid photographs of the world.

3. **The audio has been updated and re-recorded.**
   A revision here was long overdue. Most of the listening in the previous edition dated back to 1996. The world has changed much over the last two decades and a half. The *Premium Edition* audio uses new examples and new names to bring the listening up to date.

I hope you enjoy this *Premium Edition* of *Speaking of Speech* and it meets your high expectations.

Charles LeBeau

Author's Acknowledgments

Life has been very good and there are too many people to thank by name. In short, I am grateful to all the students over all the years that have used *Speaking of Speech*, enough students now to fill almost four Tokyo Domes! And, of course, I am indebted to all the teachers who chose and continue to choose *Speaking of Speech*—you know who you are.

Special love and appreciation go to my co-author, co-presenter, and co-conspirator, David Harrington. Life would not have been the same without him!

And thanks to Tsuyoshi Yoshida and Rika Kojima at National Geographic Learning for giving *Speaking of Speech* a new home.

Special thanks go to Reitaku University for the use of their facilities, to Merwyn Torikian for the direction, production, editing of the video, and his creative input. Thanks also to the hard work of the cast in order of appearance: Nico Struc, Alessandro Grimaldi, Kana Yamase, Magdalena Ionescu, Robert Hamilton, Daisuke Hayashi, and David Groff. Finally, a round of applause should go to the Reitaku English Drama Group for their participation: Kaori Ikeda, Yuka Saito, Akihiko Kita, Mana Shimizu, Takafumi Umetsu, Taiki Kimura, Ryota Mori, Nanami Tao, Chieri Watanabe, Kayane Horibe, Marika Hojo, Taisei Wachi, Shohei Urata, and Airi Watanabe.

The author in a cameo role in Episode 6.

A special thank you to Midoriko Iio and Tomoyuki Adachi at Parastyle Inc. for their excellent design and consistent attention to detail.

And finally, my family: my parents for not giving up on me; my brothers for putting up with me; my sons for inspiring me; and my wife for nearly 40 years of love and partnership. I married way above my station in life and way above my pay grade!

Charles LeBeau

How to Access the Video and Audio Online

For activities with a camera icon ( ) and/or a headset icon (🎧 00),
the video and audio are available at the following website.

https://ngljapan.com/sos-audiovideo/

You can access the video and audio as outlined below.

❶ Visit the website above.

❷ Click "Video（ビデオ）" or "Audio MP3（音声ファイル）."

❸ Click the link to the content you would like to watch or listen to.

Use the QR code to directly access the video and audio.

Scope and Sequence

The Physical Message [pp. 11–48]

Unit	Presentation Skill	Video
1 [pp. 13–23]	**Posture and Eye Contact** the foundation of the Physical Message	In Episode 1, Max Jones recommends visiting his hometown, Seattle, Washington. [Informative Presentation]
2 [pp. 24–35]	**Gestures** supporting your words with the Physical Message	In Episode 2, Emma Suzuki does an online presentation describing her ideal campus. [Layout Presentation]
3 [pp. 36–48]	**Voice Inflection** emphasizing key words to help the audience remember	In Episode 3, Julia LaBelle teaches the audience how to make her favorite snack. [Demonstration Presentation]

The Visual Message [pp. 49–68]

Unit	Presentation Skill	Video
4 [pp. 50–59]	**Effective Visuals** creating visuals that speak to the audience	Episode 4 contrasts the visuals of two presentations on a new hybrid car.
5 [pp. 60–68]	**Explaining Visuals** explanations that get the most out of your visuals	In Episode 5, a teacher presents two little-known countries to the class. [Comparison Presentation]

The Story Message [pp. 69–113]

Unit	Presentation Skill	Video
6 [pp. 74–82]	**The Introduction** engaging the audience from the start	Episode 6 features three introductions on the same topic delivered by three presenters.
7 [pp. 83–102]	**The Body** using evidence and transitions to build your message	In Episode 7, Mike Jackson delivers the body of his product comparison presentation.
8 [pp. 103–113]	**The Conclusion** a simple formula for summarizing your presentation	Episode 8 features three conclusions on the same topic delivered by three presenters.

Final Performance [pp. 114–117]

Performance	Slide Design	The Verbal Message
Learners prepare and perform a presentation introducing their hometown or a city they recommend visiting.	Working with Photos and Titles	Modals: Subject + Can + Verb + Noun
Learners prepare and perform a presentation describing the layout of their ideal campus.	Working with Multiple Images	Location: Location + Facility + Reason
Learners prepare and perform a presentation demonstrating how to prepare or cook a dish of their choice.	Working with Text Boxes	Demonstration: Sequencer + Verb + Noun + Warning

Performance	Slide Design	The Verbal Message
Learners analyze the visuals of two presentations.	—	—
Learners research two countries and perform a presentation comparing the two countries.	Showing Comparisons	IEET (Introduce, Explain, Emphasize, and Transition)

Performance	Slide Design	The Verbal Message
Learners prepare and deliver the introduction of a product comparison presentation.	Designing Interesting Introductions	Titles: Verb-ing + Noun + to + Verb + Noun
Learners prepare and deliver the body of their product comparison presentation.	Working with Tables	Transitions
Learners prepare and deliver the conclusion of their product comparison presentation.	Making Memorable Conclusions	Conclusions: Transition + Title + Summary

The Four Messages in a Presentation

The Physical Message

Not all communication in a presentation comes from words. The way you stand, where you look, how you use your hands, and how you vary your voice send a message as well. In this book, we call that the Physical Message.

The Visual Message

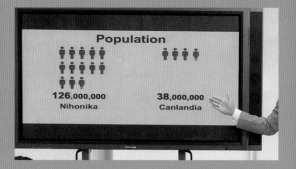

A presentation is not just about what you say. What you show and how you show it is as important as what you say. In this book, we call that the Visual Message.

The Story Message

A presentation is like a story. It has a beginning, a middle, and an end—all of these are connected together into a single coherent message. Keeping the parts in order and connecting them together is called the Story Message in this book.

The Verbal Message

Presentation language is simple language. In this book, we learn strategies for simplifying and managing the Verbal Message.

The Physical Message

What Is the Physical Message?

Just as words form the spoken language, how we stand, where we look, how we move our hands, and the tone of our voice form the body language. This Physical Message includes four skill areas.

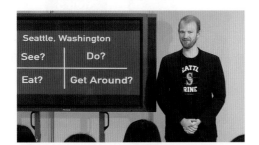

Posture
The way we stand and position our whole body

Eye Contact
Where we look to keep in touch with the audience as we speak

Gestures
How we move our hands to support our words

Voice Inflection
The way we change the tone of our voice to emphasize key words

Why Is the Physical Message Important?

A good Physical Message sends a confident, positive, energetic and enthusiastic message to the audience.

Physical Message Pairwork

Take turns trying to communicate the following phrases to your partner.
You may choose randomly from 1 to 21. Don't say anything to your partner. Use only body language.

Students A & B

Step 1 Act out the phrases.

What time is it?

Step 2 Guess the phrases.

Step 3 Check the box next to the correct guess.

1 I don't understand. ☐	**2** No. ☐	**3** Come here. ☐
4 Speak louder, please. ☐	**5** It's down the street on the right. ☐	**6** Go! ☐
7 Could I borrow your eraser? ☐	**8** Could I use your pencil? ☐	**9** Please sit over there. ☐
10 What are you talking about? ☐	**11** You go first. ☐	**12** Look over there. ☐
13 Don't stand there. ☐	**14** I have a question. ☐	**15** I'm hungry. ☐
16 Give me all of your money. ☐	**17** Please have a seat. ☐	**18** Follow me. ☐
19 You're late! ☐	**20** Stop! ☐	**21** Who . . . me? ☐

What Are Posture and Eye Contact?

The way you stand (posture) and where you look (eye contact) communicate a message. This is not a spoken message, but a *physical* message. Good posture and eye contact send a confident, positive message to the audience.

Why Is Posture Important?

Posture is the foundation of the Physical Message. If your posture is solid, you look confident. If your posture is weak, you look nervous and unsure.

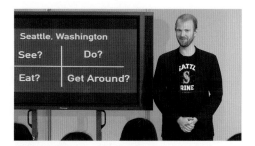

Posture

The foundation of the Physical Message

Why Is Eye Contact Important?

Good eye contact gives you valuable feedback from the audience: Are they enjoying your presentation? Do they understand your presentation?

Eye Contact

Gives you feedback from your audience.

"Are they interested?"

"Do they understand?"

Posture: How Not to Do It

Look at these common posture and eye contact problems. Match the problems with the descriptive labels in the box. Write your choices in the spaces provided. The first one is done for you.

• the pendulum	• the surfer	• the Leaning Tower of Pisa	• the hula dancer
• the birdwatcher	• the stargazer	• washing your hands	• the soldier

1. Swaying from side to side is poor speech posture because it communicates that you are also swaying back and forth between ideas in your mind.

   ▸ We call this " _____the pendulum_____."

2. Leaning to one side is poor speech posture because it is too relaxed, and makes the audience feel that you aren't serious about your speech.

   ▸ We call this " _____."

3. Looking up at the ceiling while giving a speech is poor eye contact because it shows that you aren't well prepared and you don't know what to say.

   ▸ We call this " _____."

4. Moving your shoulders and upper body around as you speak is poor speech posture. It makes the audience feel that you are not calm, and not confident about your message.

   ▸ We call this " _____."

5. Swinging your hips back and forth and from side to side is poor speech posture because it shows that you are nervous, and not comfortable with your message.

▸ **We call this "_____."**

6. Rubbing your hands together as if you were washing them or playing with something in your hands is poor speech posture because it shows that you are nervous.

▸ **We call this "_____."**

7. Looking out of the window or staring at the back of the room is poor eye contact for a speech because it makes the audience feel that you are not interested in them.

▸ **We call this "_____."**

8. Standing stiffly at attention with your feet together and your hands at your sides is poor speech posture because it makes you look nervous and uncomfortable in your role as speaker.

▸ **We call this "_____."**

Step 2 Listen to the audio and check your answers.

Posture: How to Do It

Making a good first impression is important. Even before you say your first word, your posture and eye contact should show the audience that you are calm, well-prepared, confident and ready. If you begin with good posture and good eye contact, it will be easy for you to maintain a positive Physical Message throughout your presentation.

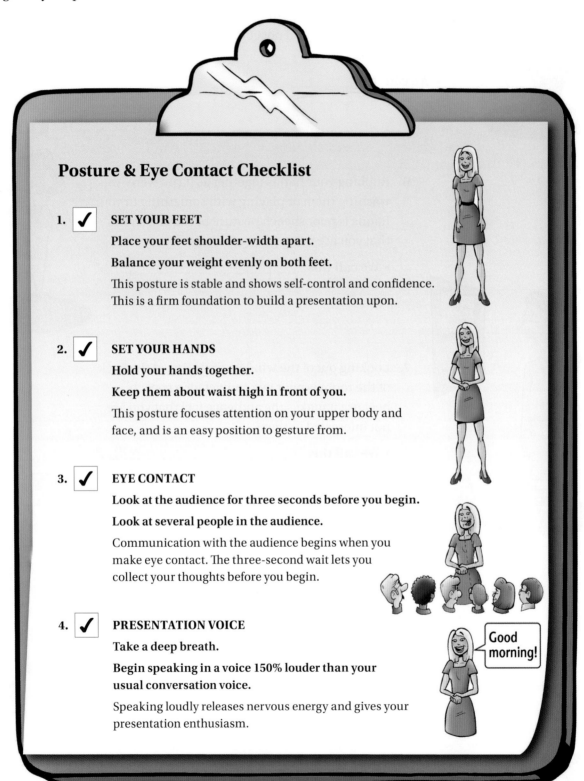

Posture & Eye Contact Checklist

1. ✔ **SET YOUR FEET**

   Place your feet shoulder-width apart.

   Balance your weight evenly on both feet.

   This posture is stable and shows self-control and confidence. This is a firm foundation to build a presentation upon.

2. ✔ **SET YOUR HANDS**

   Hold your hands together.

   Keep them about waist high in front of you.

   This posture focuses attention on your upper body and face, and is an easy position to gesture from.

3. ✔ **EYE CONTACT**

   Look at the audience for three seconds before you begin.

   Look at several people in the audience.

   Communication with the audience begins when you make eye contact. The three-second wait lets you collect your thoughts before you begin.

4. ✔ **PRESENTATION VOICE**

   Take a deep breath.

   Begin speaking in a voice 150% louder than your usual conversation voice.

   Speaking loudly releases nervous energy and gives your presentation enthusiasm.

Good morning!

Practice Posture Workshop

Step 1 Group Practice

Stand up as a class and follow the Posture & Eye Contact Checklist:

Step 2 Individual Practice

Work in groups. Form a line. One by one, walk to the front of the group and practice getting set for a presentation. Follow the Posture & Eye Contact Checklist and say "Good morning." or "Good afternoon." in your presentation voice.

- ✓ SET YOUR FEET
- ✓ SET YOUR HANDS
- ✓ EYE CONTACT
- ✓ PRESENTATION VOICE

Good morning!

Step 3 Individual Practice

Repeat the individual practice, and this time say:

▸ "Good morning. My name is _____."

Speaker

Work in groups. One by one, come to the front of the group to practice communicating with the audience through eye contact. First, set your feet and hands, then carefully control your eye contact by looking at each person. Start with the person on the left. Look into their eyes for three seconds. Count out loud "1, 2, 3." Move your eyes to the next person to the right, make eye contact, and count "4, 5, 6." Continue until you have made eye contact with everyone.

Audience

Raise your hand when the speaker makes good eye contact with you. Keep your hand raised as long as the speaker keeps eye contact. As soon as the speaker looks away, lower your hand.

- Lower your hand if the speaker doesn't have good eye contact, looks over your head, looks at the ceiling, or looks anyplace but in your eyes.
- There should only be one hand in the air at any time.

Performance # Informative Presentation

PRESENTATION TYPE

In Episode 1, the speaker gives an informative presentation about his favorite city.

PRESENTATION SKILL

In an informative presentation, eye contact is especially important. By watching the audience faces, you can see if they understand the information.

SLIDE DESIGN

In this unit, we will focus on working with photos and titles. This includes where to place the title, the importance of contrast, and what font to use.

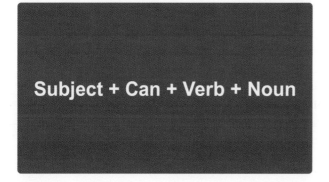

THE VERBAL MESSAGE

In this section, we will see how a modal verb ("can") will help you simplify the verbal message.

The Informative Presentation

FIRST VIEWING

Watch Episode 1. Close your textbooks and enjoy the presentation! After viewing, answer these questions:

1. What is the topic of his informative presentation?

2. How many points does he have?

SECOND VIEWING

Watch again and complete the form below. Fill in the activities for "See," "Do," "Eat," and "Get around."

Informative Presentation Form

Presenter's Name: Max Jones   **City:** _____

See	Do

Eat	Get around

Did the presenter use the Posture & Eye Contact Checklist? ☑ Yes   ☐ No

Did the presenter look at you? ☑ Yes   ☐ No

Performance ## Slide Design: Working with Photos and Titles

Make sure your titles are readable and do not conflict or distract from the photos.

Avoid placing titles over background images.

Place titles in a banner or frame outside the photo.

Avoid colors that have little contrast with the background.

Choose colors with sharp contrast to photo colors.

Avoid noisy serif fonts with little "feet" and "tails" on the letters.

Use simple sans-serif fonts such as Avenir, Helvetica Neue, Arial, Gill Sans, or Tahoma.

The Verbal Message: Modals

1. **In this informative presentation, use modals (especially "can") to simplify the verbal message.**

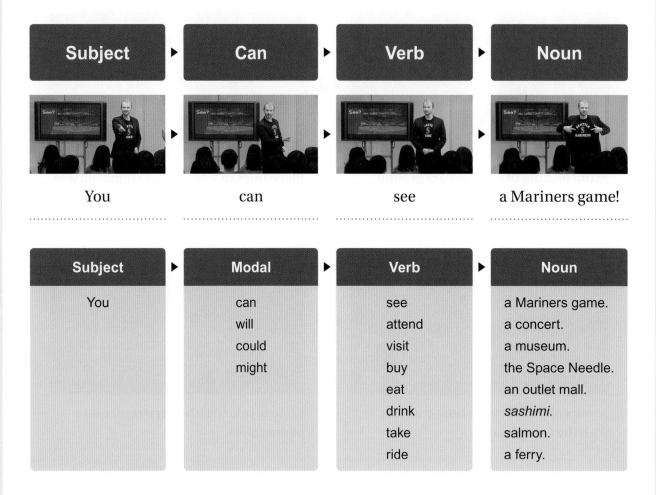

Subject	Modal	Verb	Noun
You	can	see	a Mariners game.
	will	attend	a concert.
	could	visit	a museum.
	might	buy	the Space Needle.
		eat	an outlet mall.
		drink	*sashimi*.
		take	salmon.
		ride	a ferry.

2. **You can also use modals (especially "can") to form a question to transition to your next point.**

Question word	Modal	Subject	Verb
What	can	you	see?
Where	will		do?
How	could		eat?
	might		get around?

Performance   Presentation Preparation

Assignment: Prepare an informative presentation telling your classmates about your hometown or a city you recommend visiting.

Step 1

PLAN
Use a quadrant to brainstorm.

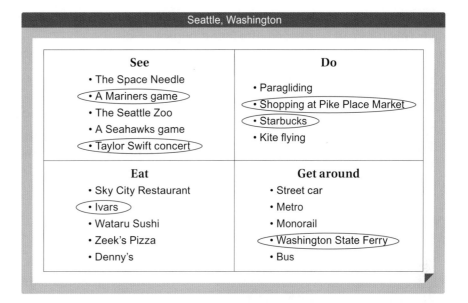

Seattle, Washington

See	Do
• The Space Needle	• Paragliding
• A Mariners game	• Shopping at Pike Place Market
• The Seattle Zoo	• Starbucks
• A Seahawks game	• Kite flying
• Taylor Swift concert	

Eat	Get around
• Sky City Restaurant	• Street car
• Ivars	• Metro
• Wataru Sushi	• Monorail
• Zeek's Pizza	• Washington State Ferry
• Denny's	• Bus

Step 2

PREPARE
Make slides. Use photos you have taken yourself or download photos from the Internet.

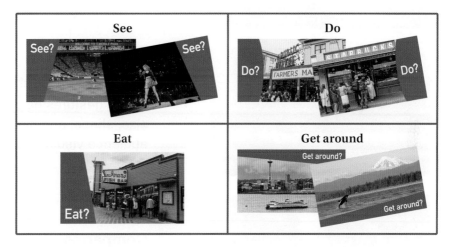

Step 3

PRACTICE
Concentrate on your posture and eye contact. Notice how the presenter in the video focuses 90% of his eye contact on the audience and only 10% on the screen. That should be your target, too.

Step 4

PERFORM
Presenters, use your slides to explain. Listeners, fill in the form on page 118.

Gestures

What Are Gestures?

Gestures form the vocabulary of body language. This physical vocabulary supports the words of your verbal message. Gestures can be divided into four groups.

Number/Sequence
These gestures signal a sequence, a process, or a number worth remembering.

Emphasis/Focus
These gestures signal a key word, or an idea that you want the audience to focus on.

Illustration/Location
These gestures help the audience visualize size, shape, and dimension, or help the audience visualize how to do something.

Comparison/Contrast
These gestures help the audience understand similarities, differences, and changes.

Why Do We Need Gestures?

Gestures energize your presentation. They animate your presentation. They punctuate your presentation with meaning. Gestures signal that you are numbering, sequencing, emphasizing, demonstrating, illustrating, or comparing information.

How to Use Gestures

Just as there is a vocabulary for spoken language, there is a vocabulary for body language. The spoken language and the body language combine to help the audience understand your message. Here is a glossary of gestures for you to practice. Stand up and practice saying the phrases and doing the gestures together in class.

Glossary of Gestures

Number/Sequence

Gestures for Number/Sequence help the audience visualize numbers or understand a process from beginning to end.

"I have **three reasons** . . ."

"The **first step** . . . the **second step** . . . and the **third step** . . ."

"Moving from **phase one** . . . to **phase two** . . . to **phase three** . . ."

Emphasis/Focus

Gestures for Emphasis/Focus make your presentation interesting and help the audience understand which words are important.

"Our product is **unique** . . ."

"The point I want to **emphasize** is . . ."

"The key point is **here** . . .!"

Illustration/Location

Gestures for Illustration/Location help the audience visualize the size, the shape, the location, the dimension, the action, and many other aspects of your explanation.

"My TV screen is **this big**!"

"It is shaped **like this**."

"It is located in the **top right corner**."

"Twist it **like this**."

"It's in the **middle**."

"Pull it apart **like this**."

"It is on the **left**."

"The new laptop computer is **very thin**."

"Cut it **twice**."

Comparison/Contrast

Gestures for Comparison/Contrast help the audience understand differences, advantages, and changes.

"Both sides should be **equal** . . ."

"The price of gas is **higher** now than last year."

"**On the one hand** there's price, and **on the other hand** there's quality."

"World population has been rapidly **increasing** since the 1970s."

"**In the case of** China, . . . , and **in the case of** Brazil, . . ."

"These are **different**."

- Gestures not only help the audience understand; they add excitement and energy to your presentation.
- A variety of gestures gets the audience's attention and keeps them interested in your message.

Practice | Using Gestures

Step 1 Help Honest Tom make his speech more interesting by choosing the best gesture for each smartphone screen. Write the letter of the gesture on the smartphone screen. The first one is done for you.

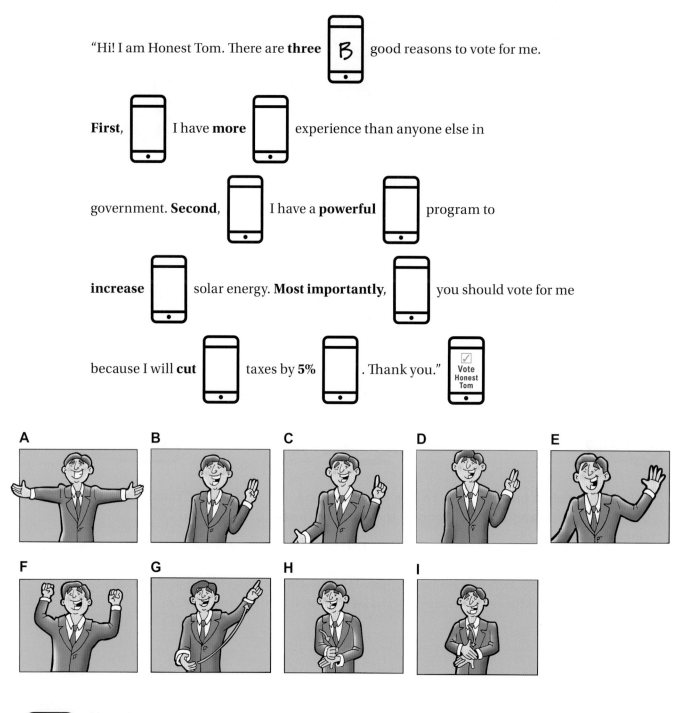

"Hi! I am Honest Tom. There are **three** [B] good reasons to vote for me.

First, [ ] I have **more** [ ] experience than anyone else in government. **Second**, [ ] I have a **powerful** [ ] program to increase [ ] solar energy. **Most importantly**, [ ] you should vote for me because I will **cut** [ ] taxes by **5%** [ ]. Thank you."

[Vote Honest Tom]

A **B** **C** **D** **E**

F **G** **H** **I**

Step 2 Now that you have matched the gestures to the words/phrases, listen to the audio. Then stand up and read the speech out loud using the gestures shown. 🎧 10

1. Small
2. Big
3. Round
4. Square
5. Triangle
6. Long
7. Short
8. Tall
9. Low
10. Three points
11. First
12. Fat
13. Thin
14. Equal
15. Better than

Practice Gesture Pairwork   Student **A**

(Student B: Please turn to the next page.)

Step 1 Read the words above to your partner. Your partner should repeat the words and add gestures.

Step 2 Listen to your partner. Repeat the sentences and add gestures.

Practice ▸ Gesture Pairwork   Student B

Step 1 Listen to your partner. Repeat the words and add gestures.

Step 2 Read the sentences above to your partner. Your partner should repeat the sentences and add gestures.

1. There are two problems.
2. Global warming is a big problem.
3. A ring is round.
4. We want to cut costs.
5. New York is larger than London.
6. It's a big book.
7. Open the laptop.
8. Open the laptop and insert the USB.
9. My room is small.
10. My room is small and has a low ceiling.
11. I want to talk about a growing problem.
12. First, I want to talk about a growing problem.
13. This is the point I want to emphasize!
14. Use a wide variety of gestures.
15. First, input your password, then hit "Return."

Layout Presentation

PRESENTATION TYPE

In Episode 2, the speaker gives a real-time online presentation via the Internet for a new campus layout.

PRESENTATION SKILL

In a layout presentation, gestures are essential, particularly for real-time online presentations.

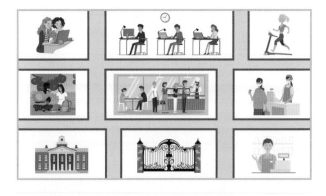

SLIDE DESIGN

In this unit, we will look at placing multiple images on one slide.

Location + Facility + Reason

THE VERBAL MESSAGE

This section focuses on the following:
- The language of location
- Justifying where things are located

The Layout Presentation

FIRST VIEWING

Watch Episode 2. Close your textbooks and enjoy the presentation! After viewing, answer these questions:

1. How many sections does she divide the campus into?

2. What does she think is the most important place on campus?

SECOND VIEWING

Watch again and complete the form below. Fill in the grid with facilities on the proposed campus. The first one is done for you.

Layout Presentation Form

Presenter's Name: _____   Place: _____

		Convenience Store

Did the presenter use gestures? ✔ Yes ☐ No

Performance | Slide Design: Working with Multiple Images

Make sure images are clearly separated and do not distract from each other.

Don't run images together.

Use color/lines to separate images.

Don't mix styles.

Be consistent. Use all photos or all illustrations.

Don't focus the action off the slide.

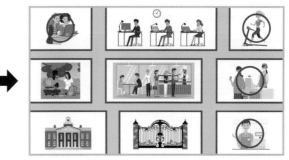

Focus attention into the slide by facing people and action inward.

The Verbal Message: Location

The verbal message of a layout is very easy. Learn the language for location, and then learn how to explain where things are.

1. Location by top/bottom and right/left

in the **upper/top left corner**	in the **upper/top center**	in the **upper/top right corner**
in the **center/middle left**	in the **center/middle**	in the **center/middle right**
in the **lower/bottom left corner**	in the **lower/bottom center**	in the **lower/bottom right corner**

2. Location by north/south and east/west

in the **northwest corner**	in the **north center**	in the **northeast corner**
in the **mid-west center**	in the **center/middle**	in the **mid-east center**
in the **southwest corner**	in the **south center**	in the **southeast corner**

3. Use this language to explain where things are

Location ▶	Facility ▶	Reason
In the bottom center,	we will have the main gate	because this side is closest to the station.
In the center,	there will be a cafeteria	so we can get there quickly.
In the upper right corner,	we are planning a gym	so you can exercise after breakfast.

Performance | Presentation Preparation

Assignment: Prepare a presentation on your ideal campus layout.

 PLAN
Use a 9-square grid to plan your layout presentation.

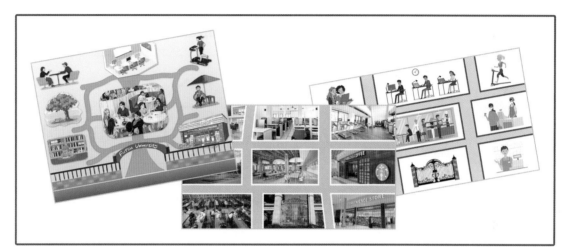

 PREPARE
Make a visual. You can make a single 9-square poster, or a single 9-square slide. You can use photos you have taken, photos from the Internet, illustrations you have drawn, or illustrations from the Internet.

Step 3 PRACTICE
Concentrate on gestures. Notice how the presenter in the video uses gestures to guide us through the 9 squares.

 PERFORM
Presenters, use your visuals to explain your ideal campus layout. Listeners, fill in the form on page 119.

What Is Voice Inflection?

Voice inflection means changing your voice. You can change your voice in one of three ways. Listen to these three examples.

1. Stressing a word or phrase

I have a **LOT** of experience.

2. Stretching a word or phrase

No . . . I have a **L**o**t** of experience.

3. Pausing before a word or phrase

( )
No . . . I have a . . . **LOT** of experience.

Why Is Voice Inflection Important?

Using inflection is a lot like using gestures. Without gestures, your physical message is flat—there is no variation, no action, no energy. Similarly, without inflection your verbal message is flat—there is no variation, no color, no emphasis. Inflection emphasizes key words to add interest and help the listener understand your presentation—just as gestures do.

Listen to the two radio advertisements. Which announcer uses voice inflection?

☐ **Advertisement 1**   ☐ **Advertisement 2**

How to Identify Voice Inflection

We've just heard an example demonstrating stressing, stretching, and pausing. Now, listen to these sentences and check ☑ the type of inflection that is used.

14

1
- [ ] Stress
- [ ] Stretch
- [ ] Pause

I will not raise taxes.

2
The coronavirus is a real danger!
- [ ] Stress
- [ ] Stretch
- [ ] Pause

3
- [ ] Stress
- [ ] Stretch
- [ ] Pause

A little tabasco goes a long, long way.

4
Indonesia has over 17,000 islands.
- [ ] Stress
- [ ] Stretch
- [ ] Pause

5
- [ ] Stress
- [ ] Stretch
- [ ] Pause

Sashimi is just packed with protein.

6
There is no added tax.
- [ ] Stress
- [ ] Stretch
- [ ] Pause

How to Use Voice Inflection

In the previous exercise, you listened to the audio and were able to identify three types of voice inflection. Now it is time for you to decide for yourself which words to emphasize by stressing, stretching, or pausing.

Which are the best words to inflect? Usually the inflected words are from one of the following five word groups: numbers, action words, descriptive words, comparison words, and negative words.

Step 1 Listen to the audio and underline the inflected word or words for each of the five word groups.

Numbers

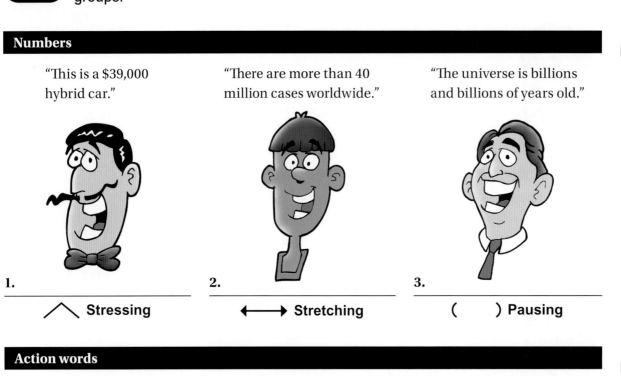

"This is a $39,000 hybrid car."

"There are more than 40 million cases worldwide."

"The universe is billions and billions of years old."

1. _____

⋀ **Stressing**

2. _____

⟷ **Stretching**

3. _____

( ) **Pausing**

Action words

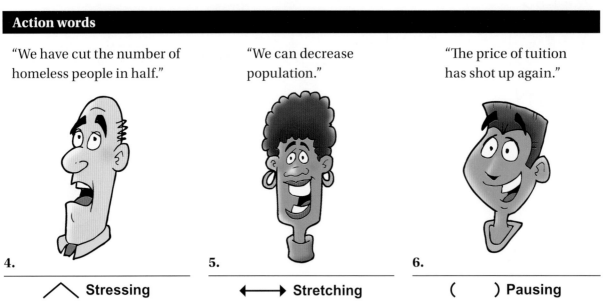

"We have cut the number of homeless people in half."

"We can decrease population."

"The price of tuition has shot up again."

4. _____

⋀ **Stressing**

5. _____

⟷ **Stretching**

6. _____

( ) **Pausing**

Descriptive words (adjectives and adverbs) 🎧 17

"Do you still drive a gas-powered car?"

7. _____

⋀ **Stressing**

"The birthrate is slowly decreasing."

8. _____

⟷ **Stretching**

"This hybrid car is only $39,000."

9. _____

( ) **Pausing**

Comparison words 🎧 18

"Basketball is more exciting than soccer."

10. _____

⋀ **Stressing**

"We have the most experienced staff."

11. _____

⟷ **Stretching**

"Nobody works harder than our employees."

12. _____

( ) **Pausing**

Negative words 🎧 19

"And remember, there is no extra tax."

13. _____

⋀ **Stressing**

"Sorry, late homework is not accepted!"

14. _____

⟷ **Stretching**

"You should never drink and drive."

15. _____

( ) **Pausing**

Step 2 Now, listen again and repeat after each sentence. Emphasize the inflected words that you underlined. 🎧 20

Inflection Pairwork

Student A   (Student B: Please turn to pages 42 and 43.)

China has the world's LARGEST population!

China has the world's largest population.

Step 1 Read the following 10 sentences one at a time to your partner. Your partner should repeat the sentence and add voice inflection and gestures.

1 The Largest Population
CHINA

- China has the world's largest population.
- About one-fifth of the world's population is Chinese.

2 Over
1,000,000,000
people in China

- There are over one billion people in China.
- That's more than double the population of the EU.

3 Over 4,000 years

- China has a very long history.
- It is over 4,000 years old.

4 Sui Dynasty Song Dynasty
Tang Dynasty Yuan Dynasty
Xia Dynasty Ming Dynasty
Yin Dynasty Qing Dynasty
Qin Dynasty Republic of China
Han Dynasty People's Republic of China
30 25 20 15 10 5 B.C./A.D. 5 10 15 20 Century

- Its history is divided into many periods.
- The first period was the Xia dynasty.

5 Gunpowder

- It was the first country to use gunpowder.
- The Chinese invented fireworks.

Step 2 Look at the slides below. Your partner will read two sentences for each slide. Listen to the sentences your partner reads. Repeat the sentences and add voice inflection and gestures.

1

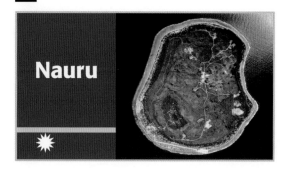

2

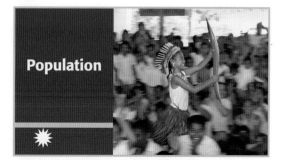

3

4

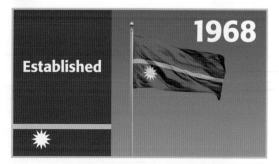

5

China has the world's LARGEST population!

Student B

China has the world's largest population.

Step 1 Look at the slides below. Your partner will read two sentences for each slide. Listen to the sentences your partner reads. Repeat the sentences and add voice inflection and gestures.

1

The Largest Population

CHINA

2

Over

1,000,000,000

people in China

3

Over 4,000 years

4

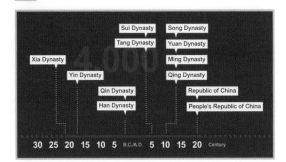

5

Gunpowder

Step 2 Read the following 10 sentences one at a time to your partner. Your partner should repeat the sentence and add voice inflection and gestures.

1
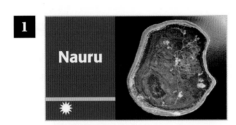

- Nauru is one of the world's smallest countries.
- It is only 21 square kilometers.

2

- There are fewer than 15,000 people in Nauru.
- Ninety percent of the people are unemployed.

3

- The first people arrived in Nauru 3,000 years ago.
- Traditionally there are 12 clans or tribes.

4

- Nauru was governed by Australia, Britain, and New Zealand.
- It declared independence on January 31st, 1968.

5

- Nauru's economy was based on the mining of phosphates.
- It used to be one of the richest countries in the world, but now it is one of the poorest.

PRESENTATION TYPE

In Episode 3, the speaker gives a demonstration presentation on how to make a tuna sandwich.

PRESENTATION SKILL

All the skills of the Physical Message are essential to a good demonstration presentation, especially gestures and voice inflection. Use gestures to demonstrate each step. Use voice inflection to emphasize key points.

SLIDE DESIGN

In this unit, we will focus on working with text boxes.

Sequencer + Verb + Noun + Warning

THE VERBAL MESSAGE

This section introduces a simple formula for demonstrations.

Performance | Model Presentation

The Demonstration Presentation

FIRST VIEWING

Watch Episode 3. Close your textbooks and enjoy the presentation! After viewing, answer these questions:

1. What is she demonstrating?

2. How many steps are there?

SECOND VIEWING

Watch again and complete the form below. Write the steps and the warnings. The first one is done for you.

Demonstration Presentation Form

Presenter's Name: Julia

What did the presenter demonstrate? _____

Steps	Warnings
1. Toast the bread.	Be careful not to burn it.

Did the presenter use voice inflection? ✔ Yes ☐ No

Use text boxes to clearly separate your words from your images and to give your words impact.

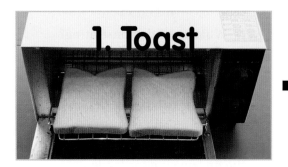 

Put words in a text box to make them easy to read.

Change the side of the text box for variation.

Text boxes on the bottom provide a solid foundation.

The Verbal Message: Demonstration

The verbal message of a demonstration is very easy. Use this pattern and let your slides talk for you.

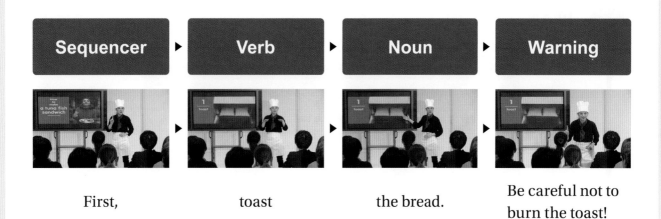

Sequencer	Verb	Noun	Warning
First,	toast	the bread.	Be careful not to burn the toast!

Sequencer	Verb	Noun	Warning
First,	toast	the bread	Be careful not to . . .
Second,	slice	some pepper	Be careful to . . .
In the third step,	cut	a spoon of salt	Be sure not to . . .
Then,	mix	a cup of water	Be sure to . . .
Next,	stir	a can of tuna	Remember to . . .
After that,	bake	a cucumber	Don't forget to . . .
Finally,	pour		
	add		
	sprinkle		
	serve		

Assignment: Prepare a demonstration presentation on how to make a favorite dish. For example, how to make curried rice, pancakes, *gyoza*, pasta, etc.

PLAN
Use a storyboard to break the process into easy "bite-size" steps.

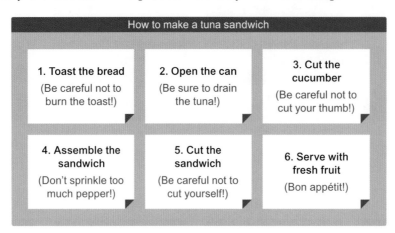

How to make a tuna sandwich

1. Toast the bread (Be careful not to burn the toast!)	**2. Open the can** (Be sure to drain the tuna!)	**3. Cut the cucumber** (Be careful not to cut your thumb!)
4. Assemble the sandwich (Don't sprinkle too much pepper!)	**5. Cut the sandwich** (Be careful not to cut yourself!)	**6. Serve with fresh fruit** (Bon appétit!)

PREPARE
Illustrate the steps using photos or drawings.

How to make a tuna sandwich

PRACTICE

Be sure to practice all the physical skills, especially voice inflection!

PERFORM

Presenters, use your visuals to explain. Listeners, fill in the form on page 120.

The Visual Message

What Is the Visual Message?

One picture is worth a thousand words. Save time—use visuals! Show the audience with images; don't just tell them with words.

Effective Visuals
The images we show the audience

Explaining Visuals
The words we use to guide the audience through the visuals

Why Is the Visual Message Important?

The Visual Message is important because even if you stumble over sentences, mispronounce words, or get the numbers wrong, the audience will still understand.

FIRST VIEWING

Watch Presentation 1 of Episode 4. Pay close attention to the slides the presenter uses. Close your textbooks and enjoy the presentation!

1. How did he do?

2. Did you notice any problems with his visuals?

Slide Analysis

Analyze the following slides and write the problems and their possible solutions below.

1

Green Machine Features

1. The best thing about the Green Machine is that it is economic to drive. The Green Machine's patented hybrid engine has an estimated combined city/highway 51.5 miles per gallon rating. In terms of percentage, this means that the Green Machine gets 18% more miles per gallon than the average new auto. This translates into a saving for the owner of 18% on gasoline. Ratings are based on estimated mileage for model year 2010. Note that for the 2010 models, the way that the estimated economy ratings were determined was revised.

2. A second, related feature is that the patented hybrid engine generates less pollution. The Green Machine generates 70% less smog-forming emissions including CO2 and other gases that have been proven to contribute to global warming. You can do your part in reducing global warming! Be part of the solution! Test drive a Green Machine today.

3. In addition to emitting fewer dangerous gases and pollutants into our planet's atmosphere, the Green Machine contributes to reducing noise pollution, a particularly important factor in city driving. The Green Machine has been rated by Driver and Car magazine as being eight decibels quieter than the average new car. In the both the starting and driving phases, the Green Machine has been rated as quieter. This gives you, the driver, a safer, more comfortable driving experience.

Problem >
_____

_____

Solution >
_____

_____

_____

2

Problem >
_____

_____

Solution >
_____

_____

_____

3

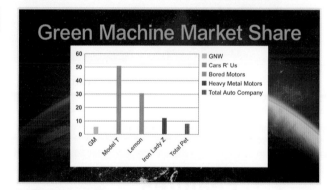

Problem >

_____

_____

_____

Solution >

_____

_____

_____

4

Problem >

_____

_____

_____

Solution >

_____

_____

_____

SECOND VIEWING

Watch Presentation 2 of Episode 4. Note the changes in the visuals. Close your textbooks and enjoy the presentation!

Presentation 1	Presentation 2

Compare your slide analysis to the solutions below.

Problem 〉 ▪ Presenter can't remember main points

Solution 〉 ▪ Use an overview chart

Problem 〉 ▪ Font is too small
▪ Long sentences
▪ Noisy background

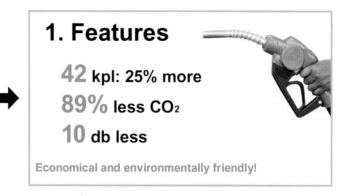

Solution 〉 ▪ Use a large point size
▪ Avoid sentences

Presentation 1 | Presentation 2

Problem 〉 ▪ Difficult to visualize a trend

Solution 〉 ▪ Show ideas with images (graphs, illustrations, photos, etc.)

Problem 〉 ▪ Wrong kind of chart to show percentages

Solution 〉 ▪ Choose the right kind of chart to communicate your message

Problem 〉 ▪ "Noisy" conclusion chart
▪ Too many different fonts and colors
▪ Font is too small

Solution 〉 ▪ Use a simple conclusion chart like this one
▪ Make sure the font is large enough

What Are Visuals?

Different ideas need different visuals. Look at the slides below.

Graphs

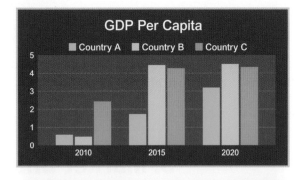

Vertical Bar Graph
We use a **vertical bar graph** to show ranking.

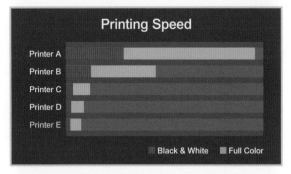

Horizontal Bar Graph
We use a **horizontal bar graph** to compare speed, time, or length.

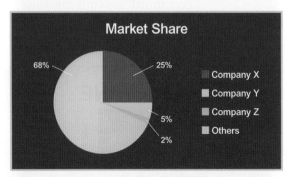

Pie Graph
We use a **pie graph** to compare percentages.

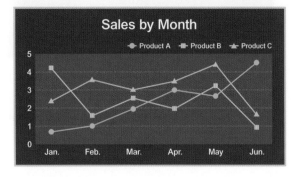

Line Graph
We use a **line graph** to show trends over time.

Glossary of Visuals

Pictures

Photograph
We use a **photograph** for realism and to show details, or to create emotion.

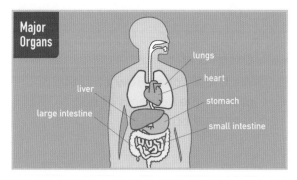

Illustration
We use an **illustration** to emphasize only key points. We often use an illustration in place of a photograph for a simpler, clearer look.

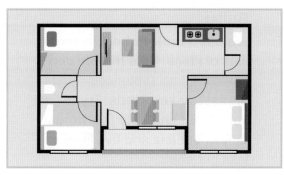

Map
We use a **map** to show layout and location. A floor plan of a building, such as a store or train station, is one kind of map.

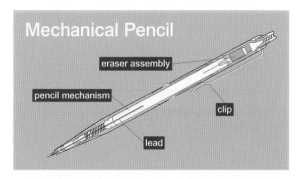

Diagram
We use a **diagram** to show the dimensions and features of an object. Diagrams are often used in technical presentations or product presentations to show the parts of an item.

Charts

Using
Speaking of Speech
to Improve Presentations
by New Employees

Title

We use a **title chart** to state the topic and its importance to the audience.

Overview

1. Physical Message
2. Visual Message
3. Story Message

Overview

We use an **overview chart** to preview the contents of our presentation.

The Physical Message

- Posture
- Eye Contact
- Gestures
- Voice Inflection

Bullet

We use a **bullet chart** to show lists of ideas. Note that we don't use complete sentences—just phrases or key words. Try to limit your bullet charts to five words or less per line and five lines or less per chart.

Checklist

Set your feet
▼
Set your hands
▼
Eye contact
▼
Presentation voice

Flow

We use a **flow chart** to describe a step-by-step process.

How to Make Visuals: Analysis

Look at the six visuals below. Each one has problems. How can you improve them? Brainstorm in pairs or groups. Then, check your ideas with the following pages.

1

Attendance at East and North Parks

Name \ Month	Jan.	Apr.	July	Oct.
East Park	115	70	119	98
North Park	32	21	223	134

2

NEW OFFICES OPENED IN ASIA THIS YEAR

Function	City	Country	New
Regional Head Office	Hong Kong	China	
Information Technology	Sapporo	Japan	
Regional Head Office	Tokyo	Japan	
Regional Head Office	Osaka	Japan	★
Asian Headquarters	Seoul	Korea	
Research & Development	Pusan	Korea	★
Logistics	Singapore	Singapore	
Regional Head Office	Manila	Philippines	★

3

Training Schedule

- One month of **orientation**.
- All personnel receive six months of **general skills training**.
- Technicians receive specialized **technical training** for five months, while sales personnel receive specific **sales training** for five months.
- One month of **management and leadership training**.

4

Scuba Diving Safety Rules

Always dive with another person, a "buddy," so that you can watch over each other.

Remember to calculate bottom time to allow enough time for decompression if necessary.

Don't put your hands on marine animals. You could injure them or yourself.

5

Number of Food Co-op Users

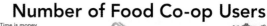

Time is money.
Smart shoppers save time as well as money by using food co-op services.

	May	June	July	August	September
	1,403	972	1,150	Lowest number of users	1,293

(y-axis: 0, 200, 400, 600, 800, 1,000, 1,200, 1,400)

6

3 Good Reasons to Work with ACME Corporation

- 1,236,427 Items in Stock
- 149,650 Customers Last Year
- $28,435,954.94 in Sales Last Year

How to Make Visuals: Guidelines

Guideline 1: Show Images

Show the audience your information by changing words and numbers into images.

Change a confusing table of numbers into a graph.

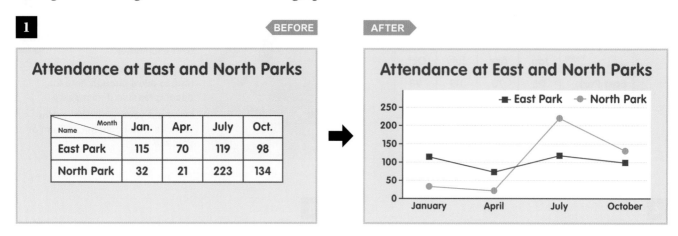

Change a list of locations into a map.

Change words into a flow chart.

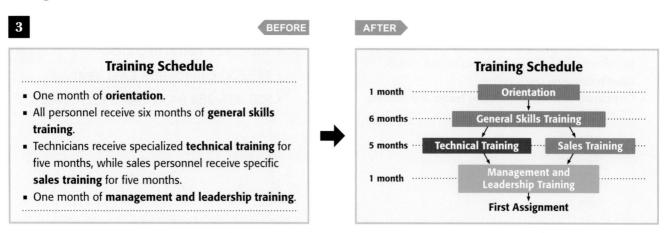

Guideline 2: KISS (Keep your Information Short and Simple)

Simplify sentences into easily remembered key words and phrases.

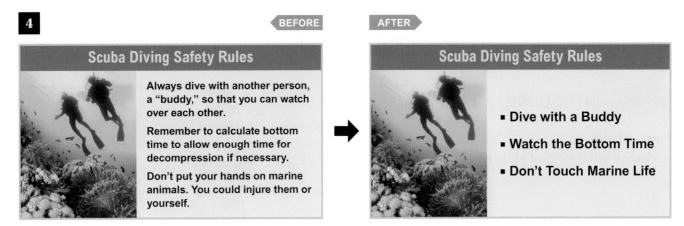

Eliminate unnecessary information.

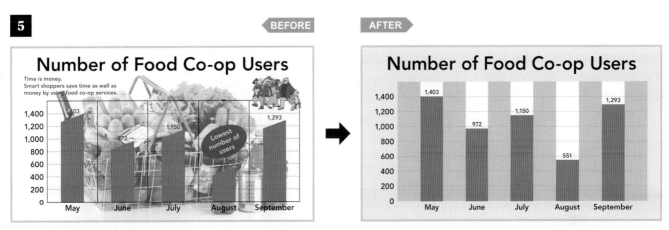

Eliminate unnecessary details. Round off numbers and eliminate extra words to make easily remembered key points.

Explaining Visuals

How to Explain a Slide

Use I.E.E.T. (Introduce, Explain, Emphasize, and Transition) to explain your data slides.

Step 1   **INTRODUCE**

First, *introduce* the slide. Tell the audience what kind of slide it is.

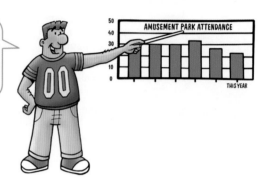

Step 2   **EXPLAIN**

Next, *explain* the slide. Tell the audience what is on the slide.

Step 3   **EMPHASIZE**

Then, *emphasize* what is important on the slide. Tell the audience what to pay attention to.

Step 4   **TRANSITION**

Finally, use a question or a statement to *transition* the audience to your next slide.

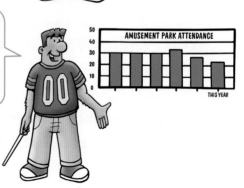

Glossary of Phrases to Explain a Slide

Step 1 **INTRODUCE:** Phrases to introduce the slide

This

Visual	Verb	Indirect Question
pie graph	shows	which automobile is faster.
photograph	describes	where my house is.
flow chart	explains	why product Z is better.
bullet chart		who the managers are.
map		what the functions are.
illustration		what this piece does.
diagram		when production begins.
line graph		how to eat sushi.

Step 2 **EXPLAIN:** Phrases to explain the slide

The

Adjective-Noun	Verb	Chart Feature
dotted line	shows	autumn sales.
solid line	describes	population by country.
horizontal axis	represents	printer speed.
vertical axis	stands for	car sales in the U.S.
upper box		numbers of models produced.
lower box		people who traveled abroad.
		speed in miles per hour.

These

Plural Noun	Verb	Chart Feature
dots	show	spring sales.
lines	describe	population by country.
boxes	represent	printer speed.
colors	stand for	sales of products.
figures		different cities.
triangles		new buildings.
		the new features.

Step 3 **EMPHASIZE:** Phrases to emphasize key points of the slide

The key point is (that)
The point I want you to remember is (that)
Please note (that)

- December's sales are the highest, due to Christmas shopping.
- all these new features increase the train's speed.
- too much salt causes health problems.
- air-conditioner sales and beer sales increased.
- the number of accidents is falling.

Step 4 **TRANSITION:** Phrases for transitions

I have shown you X.   Next, I will show you Y.
Up to now, I have talked about A and B.   Now, what about C?
So, why did that happen?   Let's look at why.

How to Use Visuals

Look at these common problems of presenting visuals. Have you seen presenters make these mistakes?

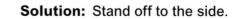

Glossary of Presenting Visuals

Problem 1: Standing in front of the visual and blocking the audience's view.

Solution: Stand off to the side.

Problem 2: Pointing with the wrong hand.

Solution: Point with the hand closest to the visual.

Problem 3: Not facing the audience.

Solution: Point your toes towards the audience.

Problem 4: Twisting the whole body towards the chart.

Solution: Turn your head, not your body.

Problem 5: Using the full extent of the pointer.

Solution: Shorten the pointer and stand close to the visual.

Problem 6: Hitting the screen with the pointer.

Solution: Avoid touching the screen.

Comparison Presentation

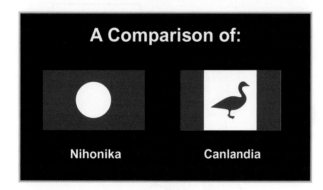

PRESENTATION TYPE

In Episode 5, the speaker gives a country comparison presentation with three data charts.

PRESENTATION SKILL

In this presentation, you will focus on explaining visuals.

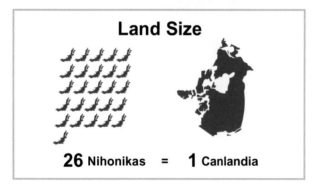

SLIDE DESIGN

In this unit, we will focus on showing comparisons.

1. Introduce
2. Explain
3. Emphasize
4. Transition

THE VERBAL MESSAGE

In this section, we will study a simple and quick way to guide the audience through your visuals.

Performance | Model Presentation

The Comparison Presentation

FIRST VIEWING

Watch Episode 5. Close your textbooks and enjoy the presentation! After viewing, answer these questions:

1. How many slides did he show?
2. How many points did he compare?

SECOND VIEWING

Watch again and complete the table below.

Country Comparison Presentation Form

Two Countries Compared	_____ _____
1st Point of Comparison	_____
2nd Point of Comparison	_____
3rd Point of Comparison	_____
Questions	_____ _____ _____ _____

Slide Design: Showing Comparisons

To explain more data more quickly, think about combining graphs.

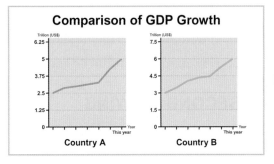

Difficult to compare data easily.

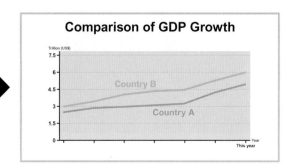

Combine when the Y axis and X axis of both graphs are the same.

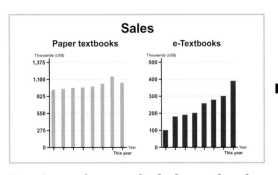

Data in two bar graphs feels unrelated.

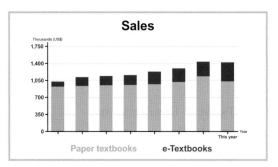

Combining two bars into one bar is clearer and faster to explain.

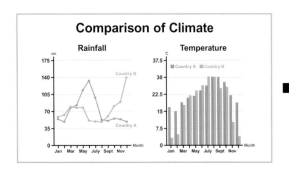

Difficult to correlate monthly rainfall and temperature.

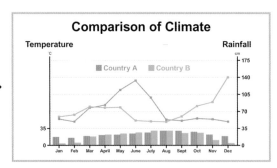

Combine related data. This graph is richer and provides more information more quickly.

Performance | The Verbal Message: IEET

Simplify the verbal message by using IEET (**I**ntroduce, **E**xplain, **E**mphasize, and **T**ransition). The transitions function as bridges that lead to the next slide.

Introduce	Explain	Emphasize	Transition

This graph compares population.	This is Nihonika and this is Canlandia.	The point I want you to remember from this slide is that the population of Nihonika is about 3.5 times larger.	Canlandia has a smaller population, so do you think then that Canlandia is a smaller country? The answer is . . .

This slide compares the size of the two countries.	This is Nihonika and this is Canlandia.	The key point on this slide is that Canlandia is 26 times larger than Nihonika.	So, Nihonika has more people, but Canlandia has more land. Which country do you think has a higher GDP?

This line graph compares the GDP of the two countries.	Although Nihonika's GDP has been shrinking, it still has a larger GDP.	Please remember Nihonika has a GDP about 3 times larger than Canlandia.	So, let's review . . .

Assignment: Prepare a presentation comparing two countries. Your presentation should include a title chart, three data charts, and a chart of questions for you to ask your audience at the end of your presentation.

PLAN

Choose two countries to compare. Do some research for your data charts. For example, you could compare population by age groups, or GDP over the last 5 years.

PREPARE

Design your charts. Use some of the types of visuals from the Glossary of Visuals. Choose the media most appropriate to your class: slides, poster, etc.

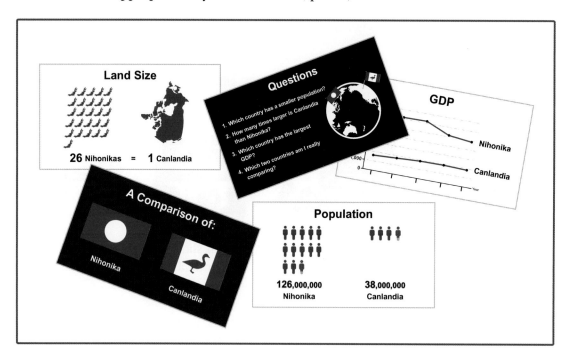

PRACTICE

Focus on the Verbal Message. Think about how to Introduce, Explain, Emphasize, and Transition to the next chart. Also, practice guiding the audience through each chart by pointing.

PERFORM

Presenters, deliver your country comparison presentation. Listeners, fill in the form on page 121.

The Story Message

What Is the Story Message?

The Story Message is the way you put your information together into a standard presentation structure.

1 INTRODUCTION

- Greeting
- What/Title
- Why/Hook
- Overview
  Main Point 1
  Main Point 2
  Main Point 3

  TRANSITION

2 BODY

- Main Point 1
  Numbers/Examples

  TRANSITION

- Main Point 2
  Numbers/Examples

  TRANSITION

- Main Point 3
  Numbers/Examples

  TRANSITION

3 CONCLUSION

- Repeat What/Title
- Main Point 1
  Focus Point
- Main Point 2
  Focus Point
- Main Point 3
  Focus Point

The Introduction
This is where you get your audience's attention and preview your story.

The Body
This is where transitions connect your visuals into a story.

The Conclusion
This is where you tell your audience what to remember from your story.

Why Is the Story Message Important?

People enjoy stories. People remember stories. A good Story Message makes your presentation interesting, easy to understand, and memorable.

How to Use Presentation Structure

Giving a presentation is like giving a tour. Look at the following example of Safari Bob giving a tour of the zoo.

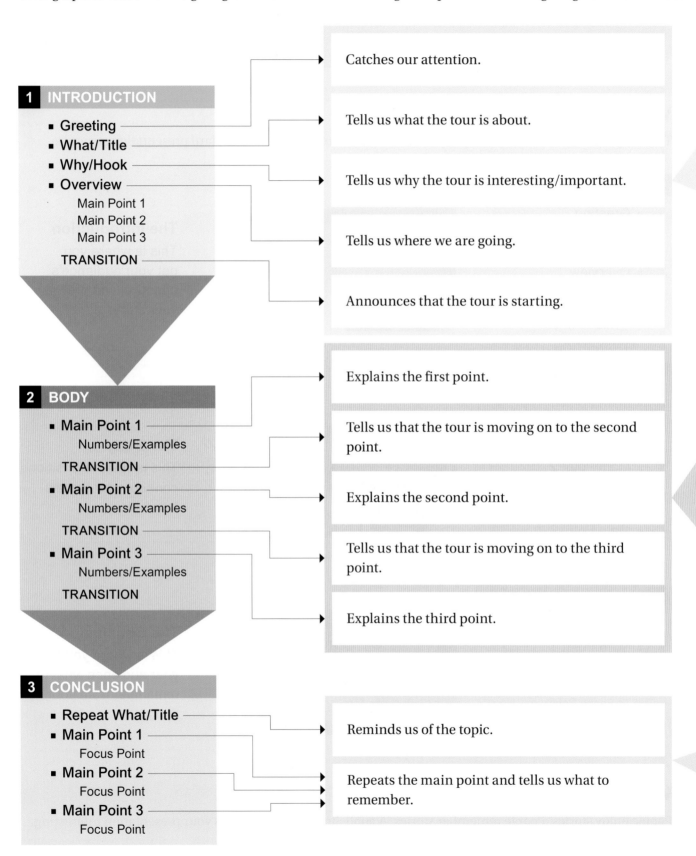

1 INTRODUCTION
- Greeting
- What/Title
- Why/Hook
- Overview
  - Main Point 1
  - Main Point 2
  - Main Point 3
- TRANSITION

Catches our attention.

Tells us what the tour is about.

Tells us why the tour is interesting/important.

Tells us where we are going.

Announces that the tour is starting.

2 BODY
- Main Point 1
  - Numbers/Examples
- TRANSITION
- Main Point 2
  - Numbers/Examples
- TRANSITION
- Main Point 3
  - Numbers/Examples
- TRANSITION

Explains the first point.

Tells us that the tour is moving on to the second point.

Explains the second point.

Tells us that the tour is moving on to the third point.

Explains the third point.

3 CONCLUSION
- Repeat What/Title
- Main Point 1
  - Focus Point
- Main Point 2
  - Focus Point
- Main Point 3
  - Focus Point

Reminds us of the topic.

Repeats the main point and tells us what to remember.

The Story Message

Endangered Animals of Asia

Your Tour Guide
– Safari Bob –

Good morning! My name is Safari Bob, your tour guide. Today, I have an important message for you. Important because we are going to look at some endangered animals of Asia. These animals may soon disappear without your help.

Endangered Animals of:

1. Japan
2. China
3. Indonesia and Malaysia

Now, as for today's tour. First, we will take a look at the endangered animals of Japan. Second, we will look at the endangered animals of China, and, finally, the endangered animals of Indonesia and Malaysia.

Endangered Animals of
Japan

Here are the endangered animals of Japan. First, the red-crowned crane, sometimes called the Japanese crane . . .

We have seen the endangered animals of Japan. Next, please follow me to the endangered animals of China.

Endangered Animals of
China

Here you see the endangered animals of China. Let's begin by taking a look at the Giant Panda . . .

Up to now, we have looked at the endangered animals of both Japan and China. Now, let's move on to the endangered animals of Indonesia and Malaysia.

Endangered Animals of

Indonesia and Malaysia

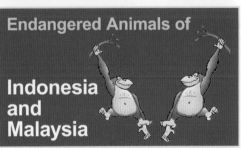

Here are the endangered animals of Indonesia and Malaysia. Let's begin by looking at the largest and most famous, the orangutan . . .

Conclusion:

1. Japanese crane
2. Panda
3. Orangutan

These animals need protection!

In conclusion, today we looked at endangered animals of Asia. We saw three groups of animals. First, endangered animals of Japan. Second, endangered animals of China, and third, endangered animals of Indonesia and Malaysia. Thank you for your attention. Do you have any questions?

Practice ▶ ## Using Presentation Structure

Step 1 So far, we have learned that the structure of a presentation is similar to the structure of a tour. We have also seen that the job of a presenter is to guide the audience through the presentation. We have learned that a presentation has an introduction, a body, and a conclusion.

Now, we will apply all this to making a speech about our favorite restaurant. But, first, let's organize a speech given by the famous pop star, Justin Beaver, about his favorite restaurant, The Hardly Rock Café. Read and organize the strips in the correct order. The first one is done for you.

| | In conclusion, I told you two points about the Hardly Rock Café. First, I told you how to get there. Remember to take the "A" train. Second, I told you about the dining experience. Remember to look for my picture, Justin Beaver, on the wall. Thank you for your attention! |

| | The Hardly Rock Café is easy to get to. Take the "A" train and get off at Penny Lane. Go straight down Highway Star. The Hardly Rock Café is located next to The House of the Rising Sun Casino and Bar. |

| | First, I'll tell you how to get there, and second, I'll tell you about the dining experience. |

| | Now you know where the Hardly Rock Café is. Next, I'll tell you about the dining experience. |

| **1** | Hi! My name is Justin Beaver. For your next date, you should go to the Hardly Rock Café. It's a marvelous place to have a meal with a special friend. |

| | The food is delicious. I recommend the J-pop Fruit Salad followed by the K-pop Barbecue Beef. For dessert, try the Hello Children Vanilla Ice Cream. While you eat, you can check out all the autographed pictures on the wall. And don't forget to buy one of the unique Hardly Rock Café T-shirts! |

Step 2 Listen to the audio and check your answers. 🎧 21

Practice ▶ Building Your Own Favorite Restaurant Speech

Step 1 How many people can you convince to visit your favorite restaurant? Use the format below to prepare a speech about your favorite restaurant.

Restaurant Recommendation

INTRODUCTION

Hello! My name is _____ and you should visit my favorite restaurant, _____.
It is a great place for a meal. ◀——————————————————— Why it's important
First, I'm going to tell you about where it is, and second, I'm going to tell you ◀—— Overview
about the menu.

BODY

My favorite restaurant, _____, is located ◀——————— First Point
in _____.
It is near _____.
You can get there by _____
_____.

Now you know where _____ is. Next, I'll tell you what ◀——— Transition
the menu is like.

On the drinks menu, there is _____, _____, ◀—— Second Point
_____, and _____.
I recommend _____. For your main dish, you can order
_____, _____, or _____.
My favorite is _____.
For dessert, you should try _____.

CONCLUSION

Today, I told you two points about my favorite restaurant _____. ◀—— Summary
First, where it is. Remember _____. ◀——————————— Reminder
Second, _____. Remember _____.
I hope you will visit _____ soon!

Step 2 Present your speech in small groups or to the class.

Step 3 After hearing all the speeches, choose the restaurant you would most like to visit.

I would like to visit the restaurant _____**, recommended**
                                         restaurant name
by _____**.**
       speaker's name

What Is the Introduction?

The introduction prepares the audience for your presentation. It tells them what your presentation is about, why it is important, and finally, what to listen for in your presentation.

Greeting
Gets the audience's attention.

What/Title
Tells the audience what your topic is.

Why/Hook
Tells the audience why your information is important to them.

Overview
Tells the audience what points to listen for.

Why Is the Introduction Important?

The introduction is perhaps the most important moment in your presentation. If you get the audience's interest, you have a good chance for success. If you fail to get their interest, they might not listen closely enough to catch your message.

How to Make Introductory Phrases

Glossary of Introductory Phrases

The introduction tells the audience what they are about to hear. Because the actual information comes later, in the body of the presentation, you usually use the future tense (will, be going to). You tell the audience the topic you *will* talk about, the reason they *will* want to listen, and the order of the information you *will* present. Look at these four introductions.

How to Recognize Introductory Phrases

Step 1 Listen to the audio and fill in the blanks.

Good afternoon. My name is Professor Charles. First, I would like to 1)_____ Bill and Melinda Gates for inviting me to speak. Today, I'm 2)_____ 3)_____ discuss "Reducing CO_2 to decrease deforestation and desertification." Here is a scary number: 4.2 million square kilometers is lost to desertification every year—an area half the size of the EU! What can we do? I'm going to present 4)_____ 5)_____. First, I'm 6)_____ to talk about the causes of desertification and deforestation. 7)_____, I will look at the role of CO_2. 8)_____, I 9)_____ present what we can do. Let's take a look at my 10)_____ point, the causes of desertification and deforestation.

Step 2 Listen again, and this time circle the (GREETING), double-underline the WHAT/TITLE, put the [WHY/HOOK] in brackets, and underline the whole OVERVIEW.

22

Practice **Introduction**

Step 1 Put the sentences in the correct order. Write the numbers (1–7) on the left. Then circle the ⟨GREETING⟩, double-underline the WHAT/TITLE, put the [WHY/HOOK] in brackets, and underline the whole OVERVIEW. The first one is done for you.

☐	Next, I will tell you about the off-board excursion activities available when we get to Alaska.
1	Welcome aboard!
☐	First, I will cover the dining options aboard the ship.
☐	This will help you plan how to spend your five days aboard the Alaskan Queen.
☐	It's nice to meet all of you. Thank you for choosing Alaskan Adventure Cruises!
☐	Finally, I will talk about the main attraction of this cruise, Glacier Bay.
☐	I am going to talk about how to use the ship's facilities to enhance your experience with us.

Step 2 Listen to the audio and check your answers. 🎧 23

PRESENTATION TYPE

In Episode 6, three speakers deliver the introductions of their product presentations.

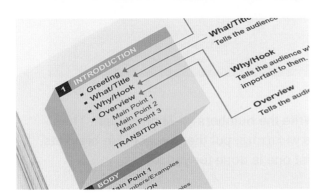

PRESENTATION SKILL

In this episode, you will study the format of an introduction:

- Greeting
- What/Title
- Why/Hook
- Overview

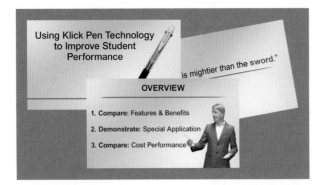

SLIDE DESIGN

In this unit, we will focus on designing slides for an interesting introduction.

Verb-ing + Noun + to
+ Verb + Noun

THE VERBAL MESSAGE

This section features a simple formula for creating powerful titles.

Model Presentation

FIRST VIEWING

Watch all three introductions in Episode 6. Close your textbooks and enjoy the presentations! After viewing, answer these questions.

1. What was the topic of the first presentation?

2. What was the topic of the second presentation?

3. What was the topic of the third presentation?

SECOND VIEWING

Watch again and fill in the "What/Title," "Why/Hook," and "Overview" of each introduction in the table below.

Introduction Presentation Form

Presenter's name	What/Title	Why/Hook	Overview
Mike			
Anna			
Dr. Keppler			

Slide Design: Designing Interesting Introductions

It is easy to make an interesting introduction when you use three slides: a title slide, a hook, and an overview slide. Study the examples below.

What/Title	Why/Hook	Overview

Introduction 1

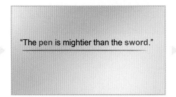

Verb-ing + Noun + to + Verb + Noun	Using a quotation	Using colons (:)

Introduction 2

Launching
a New 2-color Pen
to Boost Sales

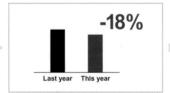

Verb-ing + Noun + to + Verb + Noun	Using a statistic/number	Using questions

Introduction 3

Using the Right Technology to Achieve the Best Results

Verb-ing + Noun + to + Verb + Noun	Using a story	Using nouns

Performance | # The Verbal Message: Titles

Here is a simple formula to create clear titles that catch the audience's attention.

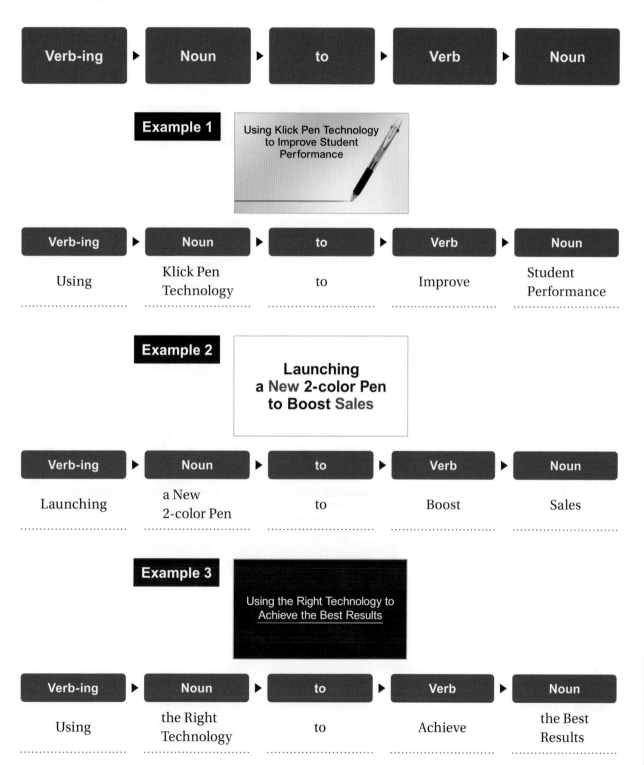

| Verb-ing | ▶ | Noun | ▶ | to | ▶ | Verb | ▶ | Noun |

Example 1

Using Klick Pen Technology to Improve Student Performance

| Verb-ing | ▶ | Noun | ▶ | to | ▶ | Verb | ▶ | Noun |

Using | Klick Pen Technology | to | Improve | Student Performance

Example 2

Launching a New 2-color Pen to Boost Sales

| Verb-ing | ▶ | Noun | ▶ | to | ▶ | Verb | ▶ | Noun |

Launching | a New 2-color Pen | to | Boost | Sales

Example 3

Using the Right Technology to Achieve the Best Results

| Verb-ing | ▶ | Noun | ▶ | to | ▶ | Verb | ▶ | Noun |

Using | the Right Technology | to | Achieve | the Best Results

Assignment: Choose a product to compare to one or two competing products and show why your choice is better. For example, you could compare two different brands of cameras, or three similar cars made by different companies, or perhaps two electric guitars from different manufacturers. Prepare only the introduction of your product presentation. (In later units, you will prepare the body and the conclusion.)

PLAN

Use a storyboard like this to plan the What/Title, Why/Hook, and Overview of your introduction.

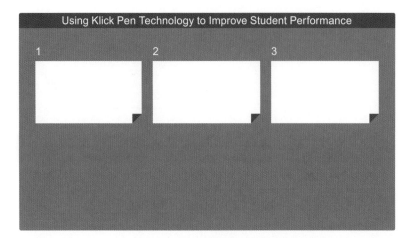

PREPARE

Make your charts. You can prepare a computer presentation, make charts on a computer and print them out, or make a poster.

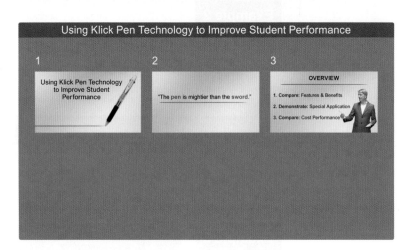

PRACTICE

Practice your introduction. Remember to practice posture, eye contact, gestures, and voice inflection!

PERFORM

Presenters, deliver the introduction of your product presentation. Listeners, fill in the form on page 122.

The Body

What Is the Body?

In the introduction, you gave the audience your main points from the overview. In the body, you take each main point and explain it in detail, using evidence. What is evidence? Evidence can be numbers or examples that prove or support your main points.

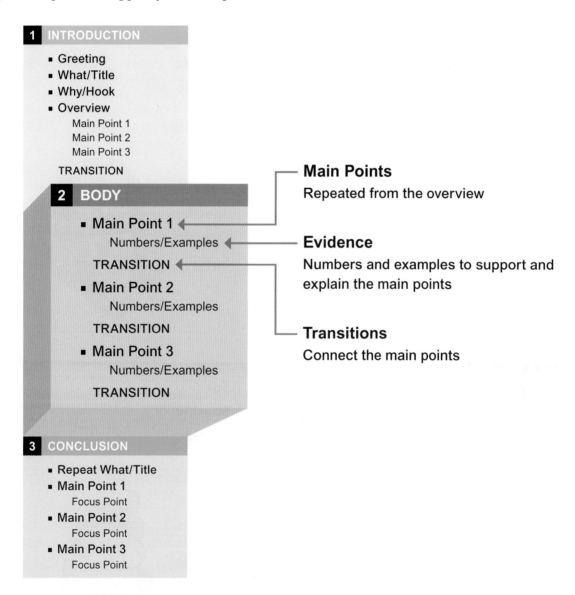

Main Points
Repeated from the overview

Evidence
Numbers and examples to support and explain the main points

Transitions
Connect the main points

Why Is the Body Important?

The body is the main course of your presentation. Even if you have an interesting appetizer (the introduction) and a tasty dessert (the conclusion), your presentation will fail unless the body is carefully prepared. Prepare the right evidence for the right audience, and prepare clear transitions between your points.

Why Is Evidence in the Body Important?

We use numbers and examples to make our evidence *specific*. When we don't use numbers or examples, our evidence is unclear or *vague*. To be specific, we use either numbers or examples to tell the audience how much, how many, how valuable, how good, how bad, how much better than, how much worse than, etc.

Listen to the audio and check ☑ whether the evidence is vague or specific.

Statement 1.   ☐ Vague   ☐ Specific   🎧 24
Statement 2.   ☐ Vague   ☐ Specific
Statement 3.   ☐ Vague   ☐ Specific

Statement 4.   ☐ Vague   ☐ Specific   🎧 25
Statement 5.   ☐ Vague   ☐ Specific
Statement 6.   ☐ Vague   ☐ Specific

Statement 7.   ☐ Vague   ☐ Specific   🎧 26
Statement 8.   ☐ Vague   ☐ Specific
Statement 9.   ☐ Vague   ☐ Specific

Statement 10.   ☐ Vague   ☐ Specific   🎧 27
Statement 11.   ☐ Vague   ☐ Specific
Statement 12.   ☐ Vague   ☐ Specific

How to Use Evidence in the Body

Numbers are usually used as evidence when we are talking about prices, percentages, statistics, sizes, distances, lengths of time, or other things that are easily measured. Examples are usually used as evidence when we are talking about quality, comfort, beauty or other things that are difficult to measure.

Listen to the audio and check ☑ whether the speaker uses a number or an example as evidence.

1

☐ Number
☐ Example

The price of this TV is . . .

28

2

You can believe our quality is high because . . .

☐ Number
☐ Example

29

3

☐ Number
☐ Example

San Francisco is expensive . . .

30

4

It is easy to get lost in my neighborhood . . .

☐ Number
☐ Example

31

5

☐ Number
☐ Example

Michael Jordan is the greatest basketball player of all time . . .

32

6

Research shows that cigarette smokers are . . .

☐ Number
☐ Example

33

Using Evidence in the Body

Now try giving numbers and examples as evidence yourself. Write three pieces of evidence for the following statements. Use either numbers or examples. (If you don't know real numbers or examples, it is OK to guess.)

My hometown is beautiful.

1. _____
   _____
   _____

2. _____
   _____
   _____

3. _____
   _____
   _____

My university is a great school.

1. _____
   _____
   _____

2. _____
   _____
   _____

3. _____
   _____
   _____

Practice **Using Evidence in the Body—Pairwork**

Student A (Student B: Please turn to the next page.)

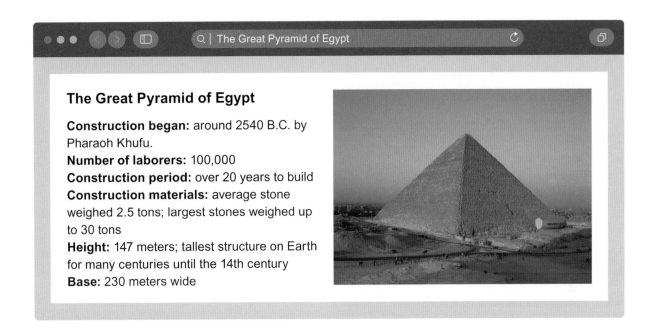

Q | The Great Pyramid of Egypt

The Great Pyramid of Egypt

Construction began: around 2540 B.C. by Pharaoh Khufu.
Number of laborers: 100,000
Construction period: over 20 years to build
Construction materials: average stone weighed 2.5 tons; largest stones weighed up to 30 tons
Height: 147 meters; tallest structure on Earth for many centuries until the 14th century
Base: 230 meters wide

Step 1 **Prepare:** Look at the web page above. Write two pieces of evidence to support each statement about the Great Pyramid of Egypt.

Statement: The Great Pyramid of Egypt is very large.

Evidence: _____

Evidence: _____

Statement: The Great Pyramid of Egypt is very old.

Evidence: _____

Evidence: _____

Statement: The Great Pyramid of Egypt was very difficult to construct.

Evidence: _____

Evidence: _____

Step 2 **Present:** Give a short speech on the Great Pyramid to your partner. Use the statements and the supporting evidence. When you have finished, ask your partner three questions about your speech.

Step 3 **Listen:** Listen as your partner makes a short speech on the Great Wall of China. Make notes and be ready to answer three questions.

Using Evidence in the Body—Pairwork

Student B

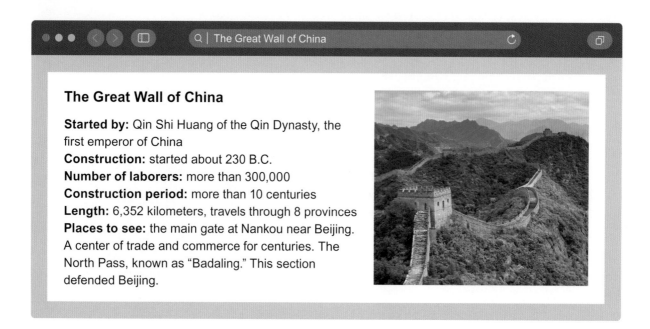

The Great Wall of China

Started by: Qin Shi Huang of the Qin Dynasty, the first emperor of China
Construction: started about 230 B.C.
Number of laborers: more than 300,000
Construction period: more than 10 centuries
Length: 6,352 kilometers, travels through 8 provinces
Places to see: the main gate at Nankou near Beijing. A center of trade and commerce for centuries. The North Pass, known as "Badaling." This section defended Beijing.

Step 1 **Prepare:** Look at the web page above. Write two pieces of evidence to support each statement about the Great Wall of China.

Statement: **The Great Wall of China is very long.**

Evidence: _____

Evidence: _____

Statement: **The Great Wall of China is very old.**

Evidence: _____

Evidence: _____

Statement: **There are many interesting places to visit along the Great Wall of China.**

Evidence: _____

Evidence: _____

Step 2 **Listen:** Listen as your partner makes a short speech on the Great Pyramid of Egypt. Make notes and be ready to answer three questions.

Step 3 **Present:** Next, give a short speech on the Great Wall of China to your partner. Use the statements and the supporting evidence. When you have finished, ask your partner three questions about your speech.

What Are Transitions and Sequencers?

In this tour around the islands, the tour guide uses word bridges called transitions and sequencers. Transitions are the large bridges, e.g. *After we have talked about . . .* , etc. Sequencers are small bridges, e.g. *first, next, after.* These words connect information within each main point of your presentation.

Listen to the audio and trace the route of the tour with your finger. By listening to the transitions and sequencers, you should know exactly where you are at all times.

34

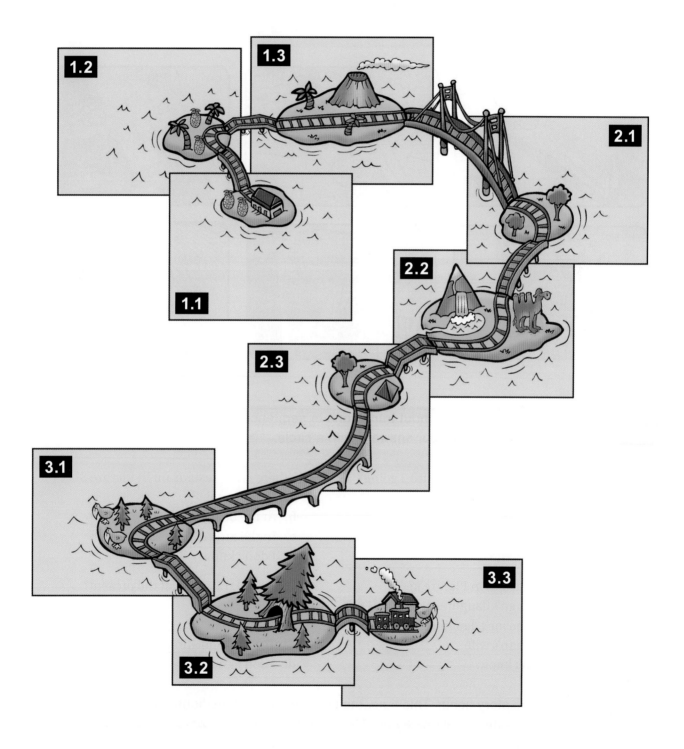

Why Are Transitions and Sequencers Important?

Step 1 Listen to the story told without transitions or sequencers; then try to answer the questions below. Mark your answers with a circle.

35

1. Where is the taxi in Picture 2 going?
   a. To the hotel
   b. To the beach
   c. To the airport
   d. I don't know.

2. Where is the restaurant in Picture 3?
   a. In the hotel
   b. At the beach
   c. In the airport
   d. I don't know.

3. Who is the girl in Picture 5?
   a. The man's daughter
   b. The mayor's daughter
   c. The man's wife
   d. I don't know.

4. When did the man get the present?
   a. The next week
   b. After lunch
   c. The next morning
   d. I don't know.

Step 2 Listen to the story again. This time, the story includes transitions and sequencers. Try to answer the questions again. This time, mark your answers with a triangle.

36

How to Use Transitions

Here are two simple patterns for building transitions. The first pattern, Numbers 1 through 4, is *Past/Future*. The second pattern, Numbers 5 through 8, is *Statement/Rhetorical Question*. Practice these with a partner.

Glossary of Transitions

1. Past — Future

"**I've shown you** my hometown." "**Next, I'm going to tell you about** buying a ticket to get there."

2. Past — Future

"**I have talked about** sales results." "**Next, I will talk about** profits."

3. Past — Future

"**We have seen** the problem of acid rain." "**Now, let's look at** the causes of acid rain."

4. Past — Future

"**I have finished explaining** the microwave element." "**I will describe** the solid-state construction next."

5. Statement — Rhetorical Question

"**I've shown you** my hometown." "**Now, how can you** buy a ticket to get there?"

6. Statement — Rhetorical Question

"**I have talked about** sales results." "**But how about** profits?"

7. Statement — Rhetorical Question

"**We have seen** the problem of acid rain." "**Next, what** causes acid rain?"

8. Statement — Rhetorical Question

"**I have finished explaining** the microwave element." "**Now, why is** the solid-state construction important?"

Using Transitions

Use the pictures to help you complete these examples. The first one is done for you.

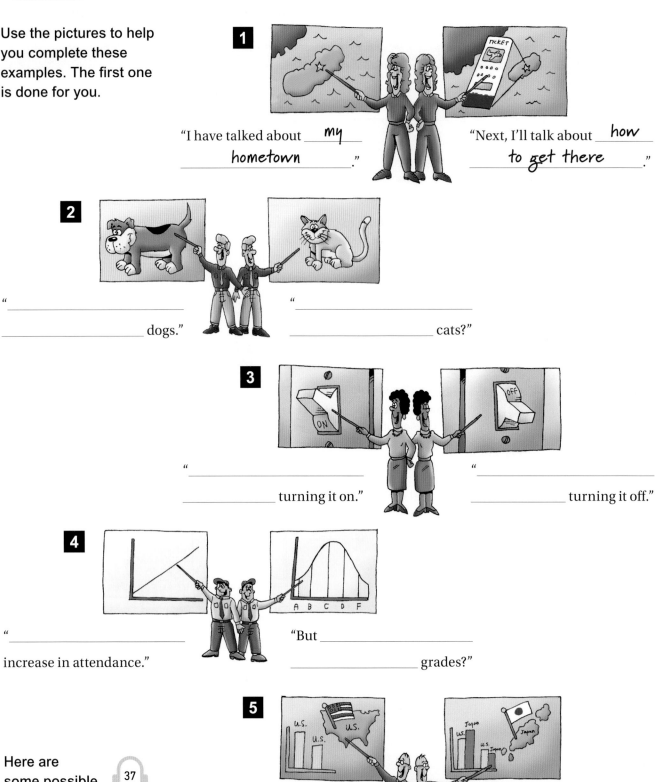

1

"I have talked about ____my____
____hometown____."

"Next, I'll talk about ____how____
____to get there____."

2

" _____
_____ dogs."

" _____
_____ cats?"

3

" _____
_____ turning it on."

" _____
_____ turning it off."

4

" _____
increase in attendance."

"But _____
_____ grades?"

Here are some possible answers. Your answer may differ but still be correct.

37

5

" _____
_____
the changes in the U.S."

" _____
_____
compare with Japan?"

How to Recognize Transitions and Sequencers

Listen to the demonstration presentation about how to make a BLT (bacon, lettuce, and tomato) sandwich. Write sequencers (e.g. first, then, next, after that, now) between the actions in the picures below. Write transitions in the large boxes.

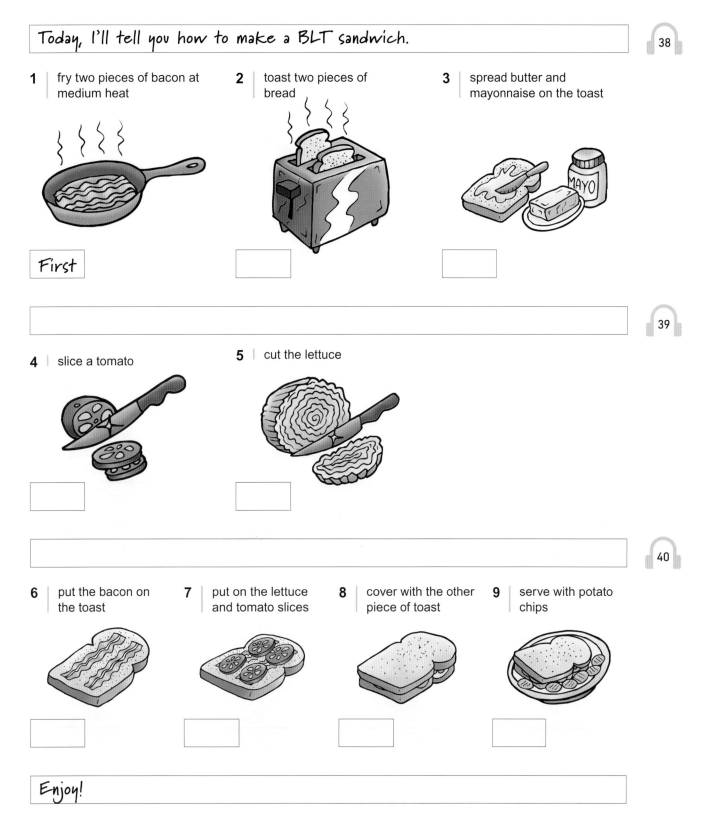

Today, I'll tell you how to make a BLT sandwich.

38

1 fry two pieces of bacon at medium heat

2 toast two pieces of bread

3 spread butter and mayonnaise on the toast

First

39

4 slice a tomato

5 cut the lettuce

40

6 put the bacon on the toast

7 put on the lettuce and tomato slices

8 cover with the other piece of toast

9 serve with potato chips

Enjoy!

Student **A** | Look at this page and page 95.
(Student B: Please turn to pages 96 and 97.)

Speaker's Page

Step 1 Write the sequencers in the boxes between the actions.

Step 2 Write the transitions in the long boxes. (Use page 91 to help you with the transitions.)

Step 3 Read your recipe to your partner.

Step 4 Listen to your partner and complete page 95.

Today I'll tell you how to make an omelette.

1 crack 4 eggs into a large bowl	2 throw away the egg-shells	3 add a dash of salt and pepper to the eggs	4 beat the eggs well

First

(Transition from preparing the eggs to preparing the filling)

5 chop 1/2 onion into small pieces	6 slice 3 mushrooms	7 grate 400 grams of cheese	8 dice 200 grams of smoked ham

   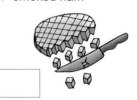

(Transition from preparing the filling to mixing and cooking)

9 add the ham, onion, mushrooms and cheese to the eggs	10 pour the mixture into a frying pan	11 cover and cook for 10 minutes over medium heat	12 fold the omelette in half with a spatula

Finally, serve warm with toast and coffee.

Listener's Page

Listen to your partner's recipe. Write the transitions that your partner reads in the long boxes and write the sequencers in the boxes between the actions.

[   ]

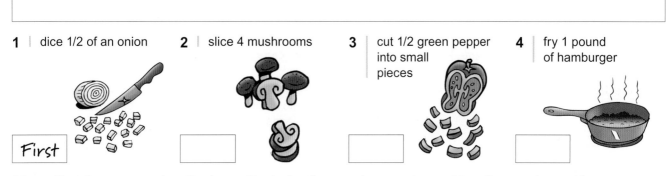

1 dice 1/2 of an onion   **2** slice 4 mushrooms   **3** cut 1/2 green pepper into small pieces   **4** fry 1 pound of hamburger

First

(Transition from preparing the ingredients for the meat sauce to cooking the meat sauce)

[   ]

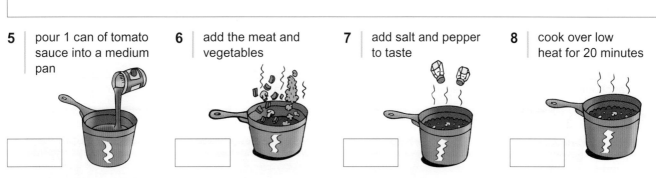

5 pour 1 can of tomato sauce into a medium pan   **6** add the meat and vegetables   **7** add salt and pepper to taste   **8** cook over low heat for 20 minutes

(Transition from cooking the meat sauce to boiling the spaghetti)

[   ]

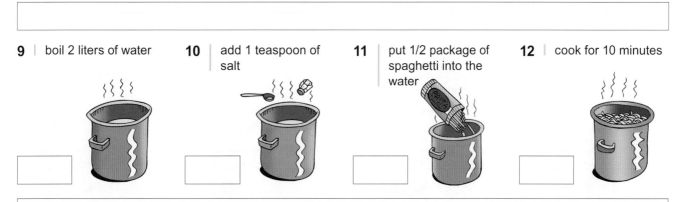

9 boil 2 liters of water   **10** add 1 teaspoon of salt   **11** put 1/2 package of spaghetti into the water   **12** cook for 10 minutes

And finally, serve the meat sauce over the spaghetti.

Using Transitions and Sequencers—Pairwork

Student B Look at this page and page 97.

Speaker's Page

Step 1 Write the sequencers in the boxes between the actions.

Step 2 Write the transitions in the long boxes. (Use page 91 to help you with the transitions.)

Step 3 Listen to your partner and complete page 97.

Step 4 Read your recipe on this page to your partner.

Today I'm going to tell you how to make a simple spaghetti dish.

| 1 | dice 1/2 of an onion | 2 | slice 4 mushrooms | 3 | cut 1/2 green pepper into small pieces | 4 | fry 1 pound of hamburger |

  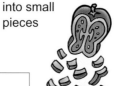 

First

(Transition from preparing the ingredients for the meat sauce to cooking the meat sauce)

| 5 | pour 1 can of tomato sauce into a medium pan | 6 | add the meat and vegetables | 7 | add salt and pepper to taste | 8 | cook over low heat for 20 minutes |

(Transition from cooking the meat sauce to boiling the spaghetti)

| 9 | boil 2 liters of water | 10 | add 1 teaspoon of salt | 11 | put 1/2 package of spaghetti into the water | 12 | cook for 10 minutes |

And finally, serve the meat sauce over the spaghetti.

Listener's Page

Listen to your partner's recipe. Write the transitions that your partner reads in the long boxes and write the sequencers in the boxes between the actions.

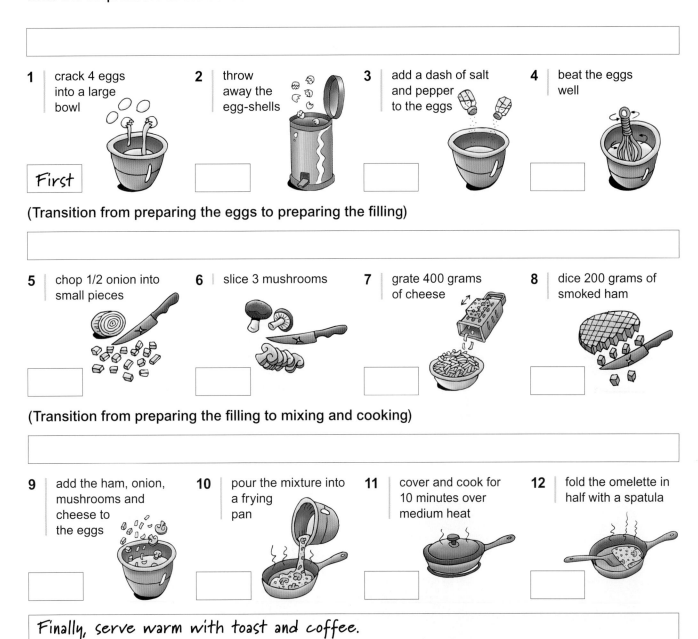

1 crack 4 eggs into a large bowl

First

2 throw away the egg-shells

3 add a dash of salt and pepper to the eggs

4 beat the eggs well

(Transition from preparing the eggs to preparing the filling)

5 chop 1/2 onion into small pieces

6 slice 3 mushrooms

7 grate 400 grams of cheese

8 dice 200 grams of smoked ham

(Transition from preparing the filling to mixing and cooking)

9 add the ham, onion, mushrooms and cheese to the eggs

10 pour the mixture into a frying pan

11 cover and cook for 10 minutes over medium heat

12 fold the omelette in half with a spatula

Finally, serve warm with toast and coffee.

PRESENTATION TYPE

In Episode 7, the speaker delivers the body of his product presentation.

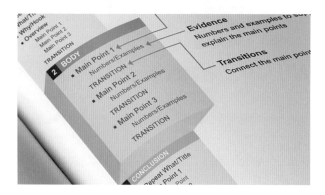

PRESENTATION SKILL

In the body of your presentation, you will:

- Use evidence;
- Make comparisons;
- Link your main points together with transitions.

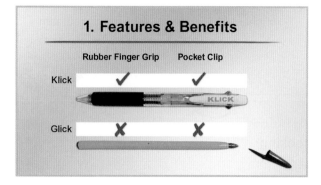

SLIDE DESIGN

In this unit, we will focus on working with tables.

THE VERBAL MESSAGE

This section will:

- Review phrases for transitions;
- Emphasize the role of transitions as bridges.

Performance | Model Presentation

The Body

FIRST VIEWING

Watch Episode 7. Close your textbooks and enjoy the presentation! After viewing, answer these questions:

1. What product is he presenting?
2. How many points are there in the body of his presentation?

SECOND VIEWING

Watch again and complete the form below. Write the contents of the slides in the boxes, and write the transition under the slide. The first one is done for you.

Body Presentation Form

Presenter's name:

_____

Product:

_____

1 | Features and benefits

Transition: Let's move on to the
next feature: the pocket clip.
_____

2 |

Transition: _____
_____

3 |

Transition: _____
_____

4 |

Transition: _____
_____

5 |

Transition: _____
_____

Slide Design: Working with Tables

We use tables to compare data, but tables often look boring and trite. Here are two ideas for comparing data in more interesting and attractive ways.

1. Features & Benefits

	Rubber Finger Grip	Pocket Clip
Klick	Yes!	Yes!
Glick	No.	No.

Boring, trite table.

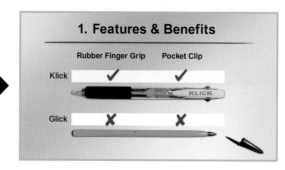

Create your own table using rectangles.

1. Features & Benefits

	Lifetime	Ink Amount	Colors	Retail Price
Klick	700 hrs	0.9 oz	6	¥100
Glick	625 hrs	0.7 oz	5	¥75
Slick	430 hrs	0.4 oz	10	¥50

Boring, trite table.

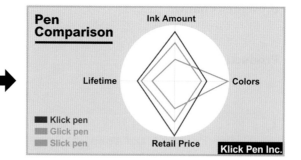

Use a radar graph to make data visually interesting.

The Verbal Message: Transitions

Transitions are word bridges you build so your audience can follow you from one point to the next. Here are some simple transitions you can use in your presentation. The key words are on the right side.

Let's take a look at my first point: features and benefits.

KEY WORDS

Let's take a look at my first point . . .

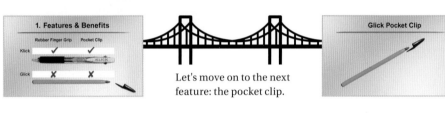

Let's move on to the next feature: the pocket clip.

KEY WORDS

Let's move on to the next feature . . .

But did you consider this?

KEY WORDS

But did you consider this?

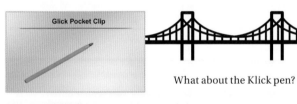 

What about the Klick pen?

KEY WORDS

What about . . .?

  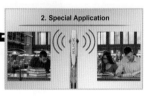

That brings me to my second point: the Klick special application . . .

KEY WORDS

That brings me to my second point . . .

Up to now, I've shown you the features and applications of this product. Now, what about cost performance?

KEY WORDS

Up to now, I've shown you . . . Now, what about . . .?

Assignment: Prepare the body of your product presentation. (In the next unit, you will prepare the conclusion.)

PLAN

Use a storyboard like this to plan the charts for the body of your presentation. Write your transition under each chart.

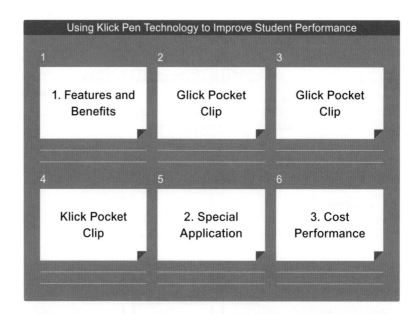

PREPARE

Make your charts. You can prepare a computer presentation, make charts on a computer and print them out, or make a poster.

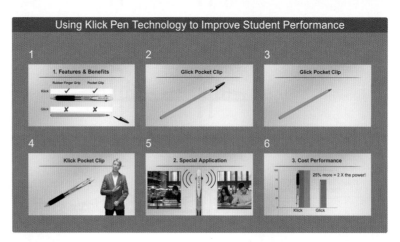

PRACTICE

Practice the body. Think about how to **Introduce**, **Explain**, **Emphasize** each chart, and how to **Transition** from chart to chart.

PERFORM

Presenters, deliver the body of your product presentation. Listeners, fill in the form on page 123.

What Is the Conclusion?

The conclusion is your final message to the audience. It both *summarizes* the presentation and *emphasizes* what you want the audience to remember. The conclusion *summarizes* the presentation by repeating the main points from the overview in the introduction. The conclusion *emphasizes* by repeating some key numbers or examples from each point in the body of your presentation.

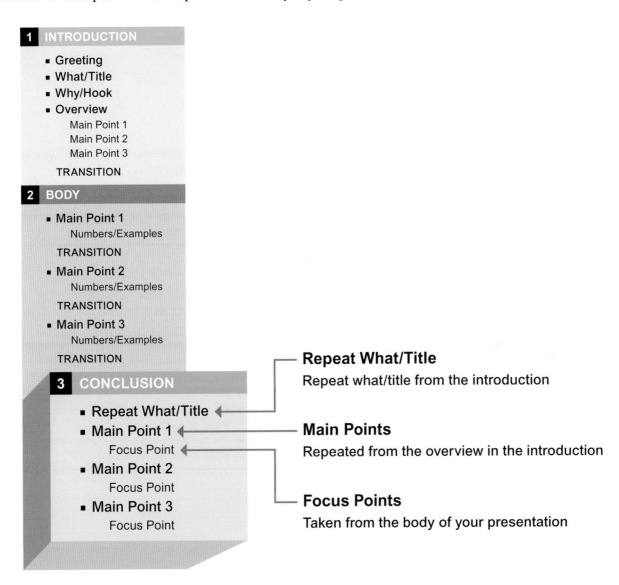

1 INTRODUCTION
- Greeting
- What/Title
- Why/Hook
- Overview
  - Main Point 1
  - Main Point 2
  - Main Point 3

TRANSITION

2 BODY
- Main Point 1
  - Numbers/Examples

TRANSITION
- Main Point 2
  - Numbers/Examples

TRANSITION
- Main Point 3
  - Numbers/Examples

TRANSITION

3 CONCLUSION
- Repeat What/Title
- Main Point 1
  - Focus Point
- Main Point 2
  - Focus Point
- Main Point 3
  - Focus Point

Repeat What/Title
Repeat what/title from the introduction

Main Points
Repeated from the overview in the introduction

Focus Points
Taken from the body of your presentation

Why Is the Conclusion Important?

The conclusion is your last chance to tell your audience what you want them to remember. It also prepares the audience for the question and answer session.

How to Make a Conclusion

Remember that in the introduction, verbs are in the *future* tense (will, be going to, etc.) because you are going to speak about the main points to follow in the body.

Then, in the body, verbs are in the *present* tense (are, is, does, takes, makes, etc.).

Now, in the conclusion, verbs in the *past* tense are used because you are summarizing what you spoke about in the body.

Glossary of Conclusion Phrases			
In the Overview you said:	**Body**	**In the Conclusion, you should say:**	**Add numbers and examples from the Body**
I'm going to talk about three points. First, I'll tell you about the tires. Second, I'll tell you how powerful the engine is.Third, I'll tell you about the speed of this combination.	Numbers and Examples	**I talked about three points.** First, I told you about the tires. Second, I told you about how powerful the engine is. Third, I told you about the speed of this combination.	➡ Please remember the tires last twice as long. ➡ Don't forget it has 2,000 cc. ➡ I hope you remember that with these tires and this engine, you can reach a speed of 200 km per hour.
I have three points that I will describe. First of all, I will talk about . . . Then, I'm going to describe . . . Lastly, I'll tell you about . . .	Numbers and Examples	**I described three points.** First of all, I talked about . . . Then, I described . . . Lastly, I spoke about . . .	➡ Please remember it's the northernmost city. ➡ Please remember you can get there by plane, train, or automobile. ➡ Please remember that the mountains are the most beautiful in the fall.
I will cover four points. To begin with . . . Next, I'll tell you about . . . After that, I'll speak about . . . Finally, I will talk about . . .	Numbers and Examples	**I covered four points.** I began with . . . Next, I told you about . . . After that, I spoke about . . . Finally, I talked about . . .	➡ Don't forget . . . ➡ Please remember . . . ➡ I hope you'll remember . . . ➡ Remember . . .

Practice > **Conclusion Pairwork**

Student **A** (Student B: Please turn to the next page.)

Step 1 Use the information from the outline to complete the focus points on the e-phone conclusion slide below.

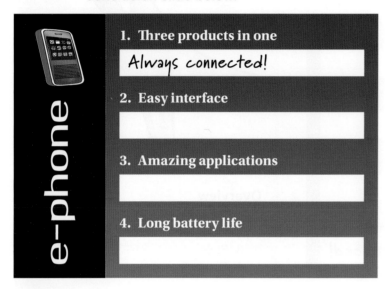

e-phone

1. **Three products in one**
   Always connected!

2. **Easy interface**

3. **Amazing applications**

4. **Long battery life**

Step 2 Use your e-phone conclusion slide to present the conclusion to your partner.

Step 3 Listen to your partner and complete the e-guitar conclusion slide.

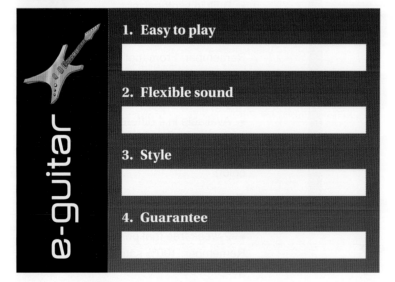

e-guitar

1. **Easy to play**

2. **Flexible sound**

3. **Style**

4. **Guarantee**

Overview
1. Three products in one
2. Easy interface
3. Amazing applications
4. Long battery life

1. **Three Products in One**
   - Phone
   - Internet browser
   - e-Pod
   Remember: Always connected!

2. **Easy Interface**
   - Touchscreen typing
   - Large, 4-inch screen
   - Rightway Technology automatically adjusts view of screen
   Remember: Touchscreen typing

3. **Amazing Applications**
   - Has 30 applications including weather and maps
   - Over 2,000 free downloadable games
   Remember: 2,000 free games

4. **Long Battery Life**
   - 100 hours between charges
   - 3-year guarantee
   Remember: 100 hours per charge

Student B

Step 1 Use the information from the outline to complete the focus points on the e-guitar conclusion slide below.

e-guitar

1. **Easy to play**

2. **Flexible sound**

3. **Style**

4. **Guarantee**

   100% satisfaction guaranteed!

Step 2 Now, listen to your partner and complete the e-phone conclusion.

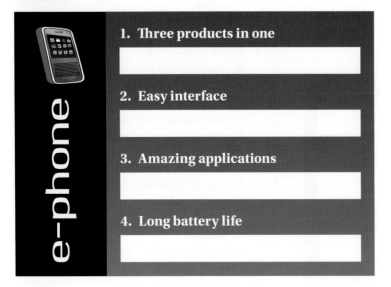

e-phone

1. **Three products in one**

2. **Easy interface**

3. **Amazing applications**

4. **Long battery life**

Step 3 Use your e-guitar conclusion slide to present your e-guitar conclusion to your partner.

Overview

1. Easy to play
2. Flexible sound
3. Style
4. Guarantee

1. **Easy to Play**
   - Automatic tuning
   - Long, wide neck
   - Light body
   Remember: Always in tune!

2. **Flexible Sound**
   - Built in synthesizer
   - Master volume control
   - 6-tone settings
   Remember: From mellow acoustic to heavy metal thunder!

3. **Style**
   - Available in 4 different body shapes
   - Available in 10 different colors
   Remember: Your choice of shape and color!

4. **Guarantee**
   - No risk, money back guarantee
   - 2-week free trial period
   Remember: 100% satisfaction guaranteed!

Practice ▸ Conclusion

Step 1 Below is a demonstration presentation with some steps missing. Write the letters (A–J) of the pictures from the next page in the spaces provided below.

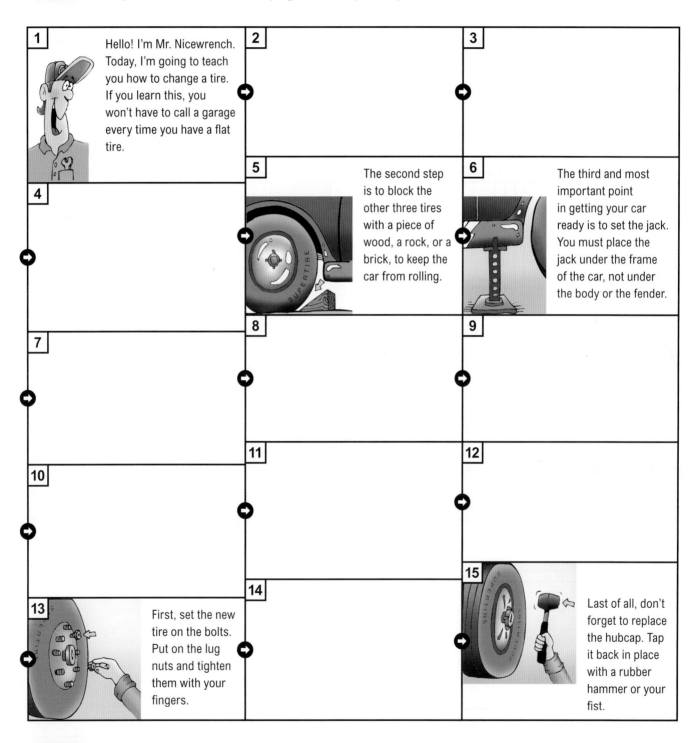

1 Hello! I'm Mr. Nicewrench. Today, I'm going to teach you how to change a tire. If you learn this, you won't have to call a garage every time you have a flat tire.

2

3

4

5 The second step is to block the other three tires with a piece of wood, a rock, or a brick, to keep the car from rolling.

6 The third and most important point in getting your car ready is to set the jack. You must place the jack under the frame of the car, not under the body or the fender.

7

8

9

10

11

12

13 First, set the new tire on the bolts. Put on the lug nuts and tighten them with your fingers.

14

15 Last of all, don't forget to replace the hubcap. Tap it back in place with a rubber hammer or your fist.

Step 2 Listen to the audio and check your answers. 41

A 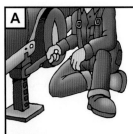	Last, to get your car ready, move the jack handle up and down to lift the car.
B 	First, I'll show you how to get the car ready. Second, I'm going to tell you how to take off the flat tire. Last, I'll tell you how to put on the spare tire.
C 	Next, use the lug wrench to tighten the lug nuts firmly. Turn the nuts clockwise to tighten.

D 	The first step in getting your car ready is setting the emergency brake.
E 	We have removed the flat tire. Now, how do we put on the spare tire?
F 	I have finished explaining how to get your car ready to change the flat tire. Next, I will describe how to remove the flat tire.
G 	Start by using a flat-blade screwdriver to remove the hubcap.

H 	Finally, as you remove the lug nuts, place them in the hubcap so they won't get lost. You can now pull off the flat tire.
I 	Let's look at how to get the car ready to change the tire.
J 	After that, use a lug wrench to loosen the lug nuts. Remember to turn the wrench counter-clockwise.

Step 3 In the previous presentation about how to change a tire, there was no conclusion. In your group, write a conclusion by summarizing the main points from the overview and the phrases stating what to remember for each point.

How to Change a Tire

- **First main point:** _____

  Focus point: _____

- **Second main point:** _____

  Focus point: _____

- **Third main point:** _____

  Focus point: _____

Step 4 Now listen to a sample conclusion. 🎧 42

The Conclusion

PRESENTATION TYPE

In Episode 8, three speakers deliver the conclusions of their product presentations.

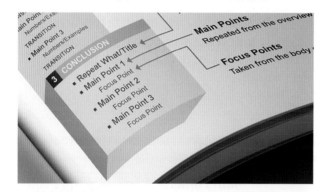

PRESENTATION SKILL

In this episode, you will study the format of a conclusion:
- Transition
- Repeat the title
- Repeat the main points from the overview
- Repeat the focus points from the body

SLIDE DESIGN

In this unit, we will focus on designing slides for a memorable conclusion.

Transition + Title + Summary

THE VERBAL MESSAGE

This section features simple language for conclusions.

FIRST VIEWING

Watch Episode 8. Close your textbooks and enjoy the three conclusions. After viewing, answer these questions:

1. What products did they present?
2. Did they follow the same pattern for their conclusions?

SECOND VIEWING

Watch again and complete the form below. Write down the transitions, the titles, the main points, and the focus points.

Conclusion Presentation Form

	Transition	Title	Main Points	Focus Points
Conclusion 1				
Conclusion 2				
Conclusion 3				

Slide Design: Making Memorable Conclusions

The key to a memorable conclusion slide is to clearly separate your main points from your focus points.

Noisy. Difficult to distinguish the main points from the focus points.

Use color, size, or indentation to separate main points from focus points.

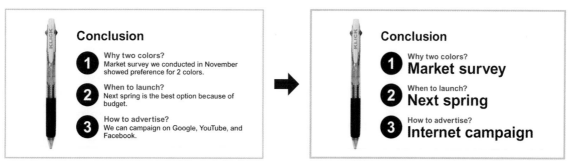

Focus points have too many words. No impact.

Limit focus points to key words only.

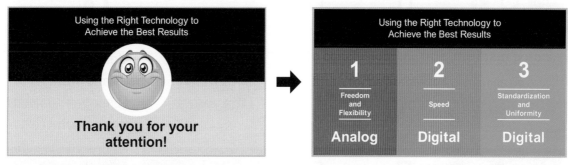

This is not a conclusion. "Thank you" is a personal message. It should come from you, not the computer.

This slide combines all three elements of a conclusion: the title, the main points, and the focus points.

The Verbal Message: Conclusions

You can make a quick, effective conclusion with minimal language. Most of the language is already on your slides. Use these few words to guide the audience through the slides in your conclusion.

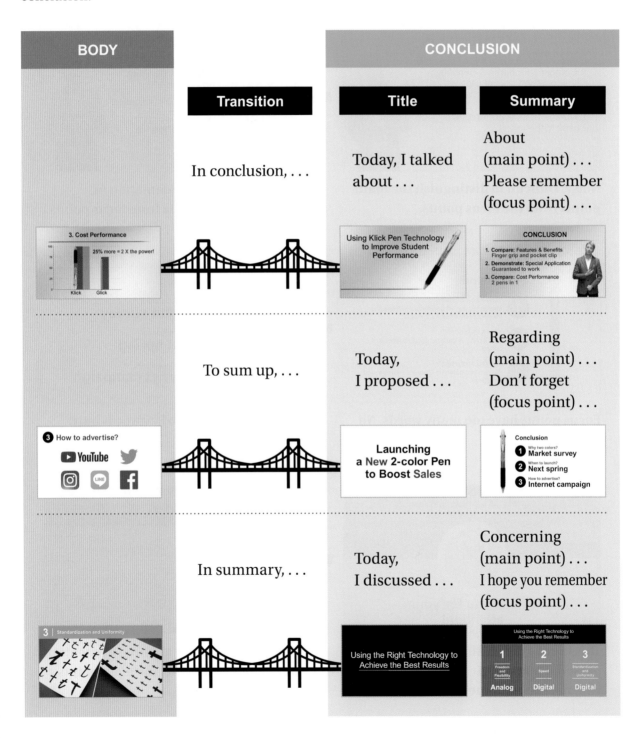

Performance | Presentation Preparation

Assignment: Prepare the conclusion of your product presentation.

Step 1

PLAN

Copy the main points from your overview chart onto your conclusion chart. Choose focus points from the body and put those on the chart.

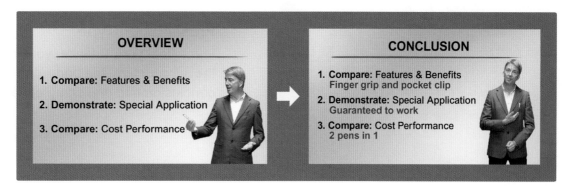

Step 2

PREPARE

You already prepared your title chart when you prepared your introduction. Don't forget to add it to your conclusion. Prepare your summary of your main points and focus points.

Step 3

PRACTICE

Focus on making a quick, clear, persuasive conclusion. Point to the information on the chart as you summarize.

Step 4

PERFORM

Presenters, deliver the conclusion of your product presentation. Listeners, fill in the form on page 124.

Final Performance

Presentation Type

In the final performance, you will combine the introduction, the body, and the conclusion into one complete presentation.

Presentation Skill

The final performance is your opportunity to practice the skills of all three messages. During your presentation, the audience will be evaluating your Physical Message, your Visual Message, and your Story Message.

Presentation Preparation

Review the feedback you received after the performance of your introduction, after the performance of your body, and the after the performance of your conclusion. Use this feedback to improve your final performance.

In preparation for your final performance, you are going to watch Mike's introduction, body, and conclusion again. While you watch, fill out the form on the next page evaluating his Physical Message, his Visual Message, and his Story Message.

Watch the introduction of Mike's presentation in Episode 6.

Watch the body of Mike's presentation in Episode 7.

Watch the conclusion of Mike's presentation in Episode 8.

Final Performance Evaluation Sheet

Presenter's name: Mike Jackson

Physical Message (Circle the appropriate numbers)

	Lowest			Highest	
Posture	1	2	3	4	5
Eye Contact	1	2	3	4	5
Gestures	1	2	3	4	5
Voice Inflection	1	2	3	4	5

What did the presenter do that you liked best? _____

_____

_____

_____

Visual Message (Circle the appropriate numbers)

	Lowest			Highest	
Quality of Visuals	1	2	3	4	5
Use of Visuals	1	2	3	4	5

Which visual did you like best? _____

_____

_____

_____

Story Message (Circle the appropriate numbers)

	Lowest			Highest	
Introduction	1	2	3	4	5
Body and Evidence	1	2	3	4	5
Transitions and Sequencers	1	2	3	4	5
Conclusion	1	2	3	4	5

What was best about the presenter's Story Message? _____

_____

_____

_____

Performance | # Presentation Preparation

Assignment: Combine the introduction, the body, and the conclusion of your product presentation into one complete presentation.

PLAN
Review the feedback you have gotten from your previous performances. What did you do well? What did you want to improve for your final performance?

PREPARE
Use the table below to evaluate your strong points and weak points.

	Strong points	**Weak points**
Physical Message		
Visual Message		
Story Message		

If you found that your **Physical Message** needs work, review Units 1, 2, and 3 and practice your delivery in the next step. If you found that your **Visual Message** needs improvement, review Units 4 and 5 and rework your visuals. If you found that your **Story Message** needs work, review Units 6, 7, and 8 and improve your story.

PRACTICE
Deliver your presentation and time it. Is it too long? Is it too short?

PERFORM
Presenters, give your complete presentation. Listeners, use the form on page 125. When you are finished, use the Final Performance Evaluation Totalizer to calculate your final score. Have fun in your final *Speaking of Speech* performance!

Listener Form: Informative Presentation

Name: _____ **Class:** _____ **Date:** _____

Presenter's Name	City?	See?	Do?	Eat?	Get Around?

Listener Form: Layout Presentation

Name: _____ **Class:** _____ **Date:** _____

Presenter 1

Presenter 2

Presenter 3

Presenter 4

Presenter 5

Presenter 6

Presenter 7

Presenter 8

Presenter 9

Presenter 10

Presenter 11

Presenter 12

Listener Form: Demonstration Presentation

Name: _____   Class: _____   Date: _____

Presenter's Name	Dish	Step 1	Step 2	Step 3	Step 4	Step 5	Step 6

Listener Form: Country Comparison Presentation

Name: _____ Class: _____ Date: _____

Presenter's Name	Countries Compared	1st Comparison	2nd Comparison	3rd Comparison

Listener Form: The Introduction

Name:

Class:

Date:

Presenter's Name	What/Title	Why/Hook	Overview Point 1	Overview Point 2	Overview Point 3

Listener Form: The Body

Name: _____   Class: _____   Date: _____

Presenter's Name	Product	Point/Slide 1	Point/Slide 2	Point/Slide 3	Point/Slide 4

Listener Form: The Conclusion

Name: _____   Class: _____   Date: _____

Presenter's Name	Main Points	Focus Points

Final Performance Evaluation Sheet

Presenter's name: _____

Physical Message (Circle the appropriate numbers)

	Lowest				Highest
Posture	1	2	3	4	5
Eye Contact	1	2	3	4	5
Gestures	1	2	3	4	5
Voice Inflection	1	2	3	4	5

What did the presenter do that you liked best? _____

_____

_____

_____

Visual Message (Circle the appropriate numbers)

	Lowest				Highest
Quality of Visuals	1	2	3	4	5
Use of Visuals	1	2	3	4	5

Which visual did you like best? _____

_____

_____

_____

Story Message (Circle the appropriate numbers)

	Lowest				Highest
Introduction	1	2	3	4	5
Body and Evidence	1	2	3	4	5
Transitions and Sequencers	1	2	3	4	5
Conclusion	1	2	3	4	5

What was best about the presenter's Story Message? _____

_____

_____

_____

Final Performance Evaluation Totalizer

After your presentation, collect the evaluation sheets from the listeners and write the numbers in the spaces provided below. (If you have more than three evaluation sheets, continue on another sheet of paper.) Total up your scores for each column (T) and divide that total by the number of people who gave you an evaluation sheet (P). This is your final score for each of the skill areas covered in *Speaking of Speech*.

Physical Message

	Posture	Eye Contact	Gestures	Voice Inflection	Final Score
Evaluation 1					$\dfrac{T1+T2+T3+T4}{P}$
Evaluation 2					
Evaluation 3					
Total of each column (T)	(T1)	(T2)	(T3)	(T4)	

Visual Message

	Quality of Visuals	Use of Visuals	Final Score
Evaluation 1			$\dfrac{T1+T2}{P}$
Evaluation 2			
Evaluation 3			
Total of each column (T)	(T1)	(T2)	

Story Message

	Introduction	Body and Evidence	Transitions and Sequencers	Conclusion	Final Score
Evaluation 1					$\dfrac{T1+T2+T3+T4}{P}$
Evaluation 2					
Evaluation 3					
Total of each column (T)	(T1)	(T2)	(T3)	(T4)	

How did you do in each skill area?

- **Score between 1 and 2:** You need to go back and read the section on this skill area again. As you read the section try to identify your weak points.
- **Score between 2 and 3:** More improvement is necessary. You will need to work hard in this skill area to become a good public presenter.
- **Score between 3 and 4:** Good. You have a good knowledge of this skill area and with practice you will become a good public presenter.
- **Score between 4 and 5:** Congratulations! You are well on your way to becoming an accomplished public presenter.

About the Author

Charles LeBeau was once an aspiring jazz musician a long time ago in a galaxy far, far away. After receiving a master's degree from the University of Chicago, he arrived in Japan in 1982. He has worked in both the corporate and academic fields. His first job in Japan was at Mitsui Engineering and Shipbuilding where he worked full-time for four years. His final job in the corporate world was at Toshiba where he was on the faculty of the International Training Center for 30 years. He has written several textbooks on presentation, debate, and discussion, including *Power Presentation*, *Discover Debate*, *Discussion Process and Principles*, and the best-selling *Speaking of Speech*. He currently teaches presentation, debate, and critical thinking in the ACE program at Meiji University. He divides his time between Yokohama, Japan and Eugene, Oregon.

クラス用DVD有り（別売）
クラス用音声CD有り（別売）

Speaking of Speech, Premium Edition
―Basic Presentation Skills for Beginners

2021年 3 月10日　初版発行
2023年 8 月20日　第 4 刷

著　者　Charles LeBeau
発行者　松村達生
発行所　センゲージ ラーニング株式会社
　　　　〒102-0073　東京都千代田区九段北1-11-11　第2フナトビル5階
　　　　電話 03-3511-4392　FAX 03-3511-4391
　　　　e-mail: eltjapan@cengage.com

装　丁　　足立友幸（parastyle inc.）
制作協力　飯尾緑子（parastyle inc.）
イラスト　Ty Semaka
映像制作　Merwyn Torikian
印刷・製本　株式会社エデュプレス

ISBN 978-4-86312-385-4